études

THE GERMAN LIST

Friederike Mayröcker

études

Translated by Donna Stonecipher

LONDON NEW YORK CALCUTTA

This publication was supported by a grant from the Austrian Federal
Ministry for Education, Arts and Culture, and the Goethe-Institut India.

Seagull Books, 2020

First published in English by Seagull Books, 2020
English translation © Donna Stonecipher, 2020

ISBN 978 0 8574 2 656 7

British Library Cataloguing-in-Publication Data
A catalogue record for this book is available from the British Library.

Typeset by Seagull Books, Calcutta, India
Printed and bound by Versa Press, East Peoria, Illinois, USA

études

for my everything, Edith S.

"and I hate all storytelling, even in novels"

Jean Paul

freshly fallen snow =
winter blossoms
the singer "N" has fallen silent, alas.
Frozen

22.12.10

"<u>languished</u> almost the whole day with
BUBI in the garden and find flowers and
blindworms <u>festive</u> in thicket and thistle-
holt . . . "

and everyone asks, what are you reading these days &c., while the
little skull = little bird bill, on the doormat. A potpourri of night
pills, &c., aussi the dying dark-blue hyacinths in the glass ....
back then Salzburg '54 as I set off for London, 1 vehement spring,
we found 1 hotel room to say goodbye: my memories faded, &c.,
I don't remember what happened there .... I didn't want, you
know, I did not want to go away at all, didn't want to leave you,
but I wasn't crying about that, when will I turn into 1 swallow.
Rolled up in a ball the dirty laundry on the piano, oh I wandered,
lost, while the lea strewn with leaves : this forsakenness of my eyes,
<u>it's all just bricolage</u>

11.1.11

the shoots, the reddening, 1 bewitching red in the glass, 1 be-
witching red in the glass in the meadow on the credenza, unleafing
first in my hair then at my waist then on the black woven pouch
I noosed around my neck

March 2011

the gullet of the PRIMAVERA the stems of the white bellflowers,
should we loosen the twine around the neck of the bundled
     bellflowers
so the nodding flowers bunched together in the glass in this
glittering morning as if deathbells = GLAS (Fr). as if strangled,
these glittering flickering harbingers of early spring &c., there
where young grasses graze on a flood of tears, the rosy dawn 1
pink veil over the flanks/cliffs of ....

March 2011

oh the trembling autumn everlastings in the valley, as they emerge
from the village in gray jackets, walking by the fields of wild apple
trees, oh with Mother that time, not much was said, through
the garden where with garden shears and blue apron. Mignonettes,
protégée, say I, the woman waving, &c., such talks with Mother,
toilsome walking the weather mild the eyes of
the autumn everlastings, the trembling of the autumn everlastings in
the wind, piano practice
"études" .... on the way home 1 pair of flowers from Kurtág,
practice of the season's "études," namely 1 mountain that was
called Piano, &c.

for Marcell Feldberg
March 2011

Early spring's columbine = gloves of our beloved lady
2 small white stones and underbrush in the flowerpot 1 tuft of moss
white forget-me-not eye you my little corpuscle, say I,
this sm. silver tinfoil tree on the floor with a wild
thatch or skull cut to rights with a sm. knife, trunk or nape,
wears a yellow string on its rootstock, shines like the sun—
I embedded myself on your pansy, on your pensée :
how MOUTHWATERING, I say, when your branches
lower steaming hands to me : gloves in the hallway
as Mimmo Paladino drew them (shallow slopes) these
roses devastation like a hunting horn burrowed into the pillow
buried in the pillow roses devastation ponytail-bow silky vetch
　　　say I tender
child fine little lambkin Michi M.

14.3.11

blushing bloom : my little sibling language in the morning I wake up green verbena of the heavens springtide's grasslets : ghostlets "green-torn with red" = Bernadette H., with the moon's sickle in my hand through the garden imagination, how <u>mouthwatering</u>, in your quiet searching words while rain-tears on the window, this constellation light in my eyes, composed today 5 o'clock in the morning in the eye of the south wind or the train of golden rain, I was enchanted by .... (the sparse music book, &c.)

16.3.11

radius, littlest beautiful language, blushing bloom up to the neck little bells little white bellflower in the cup in the glass namely little headlets almost suffocating headlets namely in the glass in the cup TEEMING presented by a friend's hand radius with red thread twine bow (History) by a friend's hand TEEMING in the glass in the cup so that the tears, namely Johann Sebastian Bach's Invention No. 6 in E major through the airs. 1 dark grand piano, bark of a hornbeam on the edge of the street, he says, the blushing bloom he says TEEMING white bellflowers let's say, head to head let's say, with whispering little headlets let's say and how they touch each other namely TEEMING : ironing coiffures, with white hands body to body, he says, filament to filament in the cup in the glass, so the little music book with pink protective cover, right? flood of tears let's say, he says, TEEMING let's say, he says, the tears the toothlets namely suckling piglets .... Judas-thinkers and -turnkeys sheet music fiery rain, the green verbena of the heavens' banks, heavens' little grass of springtide &c.
Blown-out foehnlets, how mouthwatering

17.3.11

oh my heart this thunder-hutch ach my heart this henchman
what a play of clouds (1) says he, what a songbook (1)
Schneelein's Credenza .... Bird unwrinkled 2
small white stones underbrush in the flowerpot Susanne B.
Flora on its way she says little cherry-red tatters on the counter
breakfast table dark grapes blissful bird: you cross the clangorous
airs, the cloudy sky—   blown-out foehnlet there is a red
banner on the sand (crying) storm warning red stuff on the banks
how the wind is blowing fennel orgy, 1 ivy leaf ("embroidering")
in my hand fabulous grasses suddenly Cy Twombly's ro-
ses on the windowsill little soul of the rosy dawn glittering
deadwood veil of tears

21.3.11

> "I'm not in a good mood, but not
> fed up, either .... it just came over me,
> last night, on the summit"
> Guilhem de Poitiers, German translation
> Thomas Kling

[handwritten left: a continuation (?) of a continuation of quote.]

and in the Rax such a rush of rubbish, "fished from the rubbish,"
says Thomas Kling, on the summit then sound-violets were so
mouthwatering, disastrous the morning scribbling *[handwritten: juxtaposition]*
the ballad of the thrush and the fireboy in the west—2 sm. pebbles
and underbrush in the flowerpot pitter-patter at night my *[handwritten left: lost, ...ectable]* *[handwritten right: floral impact! influence]*
    pattering through the allium copses *[handwritten: copse! corpses?]*
corporeal copse white bellflower's tufts wilted faded *[handwritten right: explained]*
I wreathlet Leidenfrost's body (= the lane here / rosy foliage) ....
like fasces ⊖ flambeau am so fascinated by these green tongue-
leaflets in strangers' gardens lisping salivating exhibiting sucking
hard sugar sticks rock candy)(mine tongue is a rose petal early spring :
blissful vocables, my limbs touching)—
the anemones sigh lilac, white, 1 Patscherkofel pines for
the wild world shines

22.3.11

[handwritten: SPRING]

13

Letter to ++++++++++
steamy Phoebus wings unfurling visit Napoleon eter-
nal unrest (seedy) : peering out from the earth peering, that is to say,
unfurling, the armlets of the baby's breath, my finger
running along the edges of your newest collage &c. : "little goldfeet
or godfeet, foxy, gray," I sometimes sit
for hours on my rod/skirt/or jacket, snowing
to myself, namely BLOSSOMSNOW, sm. songbird thrush-
song rain-decayer how it cries, when eyes shine, writes Elke
Erb, under-brush of the atlas, you albatross, herringbones
  on your cheek you are ....
....

23.3.11

"eternal unrest" (handwritten, right margin)

What is left unsaid, or her no complete way of conveying? (handwritten)

Diminutives, let's say. The head of the lamb (slaughtered) : cake, beneath the blue tatterlets of the heavens, portal, cavities of the body crying, tatterlets lamenting to the heavens, sepia, where the birds with their stiff thin handlets claw spring branches : 1 dry gnarled handlet (violets and Valérie) : arthritis, let's say. While bent slumped spit like cellophane on the linoleum floor where sugar loaves I mean horizons are tied down, little bird's claw = violet's Valérie, and how the little songbird's claw bends / winds around the little branch, and twitters while arias sweet its throat exudes &c., namely FREEZINGS of the heart, tatterlets of the heart, blue, and how he hurries after me saying, You look so much like ++++++++++ and I say, I am her. Little bird's breast heaving : the heavens' greenery namely, the lamb cake, &c. My soul is already sloughing off its skin I mean I am flayed on the insides of my arms, lambs are carved from the skin, tatterlets of the heavens, early spring's sorrow

26.3.11

this little bird birdlet with the trumpet namely in the morning's rainshower oh woe is my heart like tears on the windowpane pearls April &c., scurrying through dreams, Satie's sufi-song, Cretan stones on my heart as I recognize meadows rivers woods years ago in the roar of the wind and hand in hand, the crane's white feet little leaf the rose's inflammation, the blushing bloom and how it <u>blazed</u> in the heart am cocooned in the forest feathers little fingers, kissed the first green leaflet behind the park fence woodlark wild dove siskin in my naivete. Stepping on the blue cloth belt my god-brain—whispered LAPIN to the RABBIT or <u>detonated</u> bunny, such little birds birdlets chortling (peering) or when this Romi <u>sleeps/slips along</u> I mean her shadow looms, the wind blows .... the Thaya namely had been smoothed over had nosed in the meadow &c., blown-out warm foehnlet how mouthwatering

27.3.11

green lacewing, torn 1 veil Bernadette H., back then dark daubs
of fir trees while the needles of the forest in which I had gotten lost
flung themselves down on meandering woodland
paths marbled with motionless = rigid
deer while the forest birdlets in the DADA woods namely
the timid, animals, namely tears contorted to flowers, the
valley toppled into me &c., while corporeal correspondence = Plexiglas
of my skin imploringly, years ago like dark droplets
from the fir and in the meantime
glory or gloire

29.3.11

little leaf from green springtide I mean
a dream of roommates, corrupts such
a heavy heart : can shake paws, I believe magnolia tree
on ancient instruments, and a bit breathless on waking = a little
pitter-patter, crying, something comes to me, in the yellow music book
Letter to ++++++++++ (in the yellow music book with plastic cover),
a little pitter-pattering, crying, no one lets me sleep late, "o sole
mio," little leaf from green springtide I mean ....

(and although the piece of bread had fallen on the floor (by the
elevator doors), she ate it, there, by the elevator doors, finely
wreathed in flowing tresses she snatched up the bread from the
floor and wolfed it)

30.3.11

o star in the eye of the nightingale star rosy-headed o thistle that I
your soul- and mock-bite that I this little trumpery from springtide,
that I underbrush and small stone in the flowerpot little leaf from
green springtide or moonlight in the dark blue night, namely
SAIL out to its shine, pansy where I kneel kissing it <u>April's naked
breeze</u> so damp hair in open car cherry blossoms in strangers' gar-
dens ("may I kiss you?") thistle-head the fleeting hardwood I
mean the forest birds <u>rouging</u> robin redbreast, these

dewdrops of beauty, I wear rabbit fur I wear a BUNNY on my
pale skin, so pallid ravishing goats anemones and snakebites that
I your soul- and mock-bite where little rose-heads <u>in a trice</u>, you
will arise my heart in a trice, Mahler's second

imploringly back then like dark drops from a fir tree &c., your letters
so veiling and peering, peering out from the earth namely unfurling
traces of baby's-breath, "gold-feet foxy" l blossomsnow imploringly
namely with the wood-dove's flutter .... how the wind

blows   <u>something</u>
<u>comes to me</u>

3.4.11

to my belov'ed Cupido's.   Overnight

the white hawthorn's stemlet in the glass, namely through <u>the vocables</u>
<u>spring</u>, 1 drop 1 petal, weeping panicle 1 dew 1
stemlet = underbrush 1 withered white hawthorn worried I will be
disturbed .... <u>the mama of the deep</u>
<u>rosy-fingered</u> tomorrow is communion, the lianas violas <u>hacked-off</u>
<u>hand</u> buried by garden violets low-flying swallows <u>little</u>
<u>trout</u> ("sleepless scenery"), wind agitates hemlock
<u>to my belov'ed Cupido's.</u>
Kiss-landscape : panicle in glass, bird-heart's flutter in
blossomsnow *MY LITTLE TROUT*, I say, <u>my little trout</u>—my
little rose-head I say my little trout ....
(this wafting, namely with half-open window drinking in
air with eyes closed this taking wing to the fortress = heaven
rouging stammering while the sheet on which I write flut-
ters up : naked breeze)

7.4.11

ravishing visitations or a slice of Samuel, kisses of the hidden beloved little leaf from green springtide field-hedges, _oh, to my belov'ed Cupido's_. Heart cherries days, after heart cherries days eyeing : after fringes clouds and eyelets of these sweet heart cherries days, hurrying past that cafe in which he'd sunk down back then as enormous exhaustion &c., I mean he broke down in the aroma of spring little gullet inmost sensation while the heart cherries days : little forest bird in DADA airs and imploringly with folded hands (namely 1 PUNK boyphriend in the "Drechsler" staring into the OPEN : Andreas O.), and sitting on the little wall, wolfing down Persian bread, chewing like little pigeons with their little craws and suchlike. _To my belov'ed Cupido's_ in a trice, rouging so firmament = fortress that I your soul- and mock-thunderstorm : in consideration of the out-and-about souls sunk me sinking in them, sleuthing like Helmut M. with HIGHNESS, scouting after these souls sceneries in this sweet April = "süszen April" when the horizon's fests in their bluenesses shuddered namely the bumblebee in the morning : (if you would be so kind as to let her sleep by my side)

8.4.11

have driven death from the bushes at night namely siskin <u>in a trice</u> &c., and heavily from sleep = ripped from sleep by imagination at midnight, gave Father a kiss gave Mother a kiss roamed through woods drank rain from my hands = from a bowl, squirrel at the spring, so the two sm. shakos fashioned from newspaper I mean motionless by Theophil Spoerri's side while motionless Phoebus penetrates my eyes namely blinds them while these little grass you know these mats of daisies poured out milk of April in strangers' gardens did you see them poured-out breasts and heavily from sleep, muerte : death, <u>death from the bushes</u> ++++++++++ shepherd's bagpipe later then dewing dancing tender breeze <u>that puffs away the must</u> like the spit from me and seeping "beautiful, sobbing, high-geared .." (Richard Brautigan)—where meadows with daisies draped all over them, and <u>strewn</u> where these meadows with white flowers and tears = <u>metaphors</u> in the river's wetlands the song of the nightingale namely at midnight and morning rain, Joan Miró, o like thistles and rose blossoms the throat of the privet = bitter sip and seeming-bite (violins from your hands your chest your tongue, and kissing me with your eyes open, like so, <u>siskin in the boughs</u>)   in a trice, &c.

10.4.11

in the lane lies the Passion lies the passionflower lies the grove windflower lies the lady's-smock is near death in the lane is withered the passionflower is withered the liverwort is withered the little white violet is near death is destined for death I walk into and out of the meadows did I pick you up out of the dust ++++++++++ <u>in a trice the cello address</u> this child of rosy dawns like my pleas bills and coos rosy-red my goldfinch <u>Passion paschal pinx</u>.

14.4.11

on I voice : on I mignonette green this branchlet this blossom this
instant of a teardrop in your eye this raining in your voice swept
forth by spring this scent of white tears this scent of whiteness this
white of spring of voice this little white bell of April (= Fratres)
this whiteness of little bells = Fratres this whisper of voice this
whisper from the vineyard ("April") these twigs little bells of April
swept away trembling delphinium cress lungwort Bach's Virgin
chorales &c. disheveled little bird April violin handbooklet April
naked this soul weighted with sleep (= "Fratres") ach your voice
+++++++++++ white from spring white from April spring's twigs
opened and blossom-amble where the plumed

14.4.11

you my French pretender early spring's hippie in the glass "Aben-dempfindung an Laura" twiggy branchlet in the glass or 2nd blossom-amble, I saw in the fruit bowl this tiny spider that spooked me SCURRYING AWAY however she vanished I mean maybe she hid without ++++++++++ I mean she kept appearing anew in my goddess = memory namely heavy with sleep the plumed and chirped almost inaudibly in the early morning, so that I pressed my ear to the window, one wanted, peculiar, to think of a fruit bowl the deep grotto or goddess of the green crepe paper, in my tears underbrush : zoomed in like a heavy hand over breast rotted dreams 5 o'clock in the morning and that it glowed at all (pinxit and thrush) the little leaf eyeing in the glass in the brackish water sawn nocturne by Gabriel Fauré &c.

(mignonette, and the cuckoo skits long-running in the ash trees)

17.4.11

wishing that someone perhaps a white raven

would bring breakfast to me in bed I mean Rilke's verses the bare

shoulder of the verses white and tripped with a tray to my

bed while the golden fan of dawn sun as in

Barcelona the boyfriend *my belov'ed Cupido's* ++++++++++

the branchlets in the moon grown wild tussled branchlet riverlet

of the beyond bitter flavor of the privet and so

the siskin flies about twitters and builds its nest deep

grotto of the green hillside like siskin in meadows and bushes
    and brooks

dewdrops beauty sawn leaflet namely <u>shooing</u>

<u>greenery</u> &c.

<u>and suddenly one recognized the boyfriend's alphabet</u>

19.4.11

fly or flee (I) 3 wild roses in deep
grotto I plunge into purple lilacs and shimmering tears
fly or flee (I) Fauré's études in deep
grotto green shimmering crepe paper namely portrait
of rustling mead fly or flee (I) branchlet
grown wild in spring moon &c., fly or flee (I)
deep grotto green shimmering lake's fly or flee (I)
Fauré's rose petals (études) fly or flee (I) rose
petals disclosing I kiss and snitch in deep
Fauré or gorse while 1 bolt of sunbeam mornings 1
beam of bolt from sky to earth that 1 deep grotto I
mean the portrait of emerald escape namely in a trice
(whimpering servitude) Thursday of Mysteries namely Fauré's
13 nocturnes : studies (études) in a deep green grotto
    in tears +++++++++
in deep waters the plumed the Easterly lam-
entations (even like strands of hair into my face) or chic &c.
am thunderstruck 1 goldfinch stammering

21.4.11

1 rose-whiff : classical verse :
and bedded down on green stones the green branchlets tender bro-
ken we bedded down on green branches on that Mayday on
the branches it was in those fields woods the little birds
in the woods sang you were wearing the Scottish
(cravat) it was 1 green day we bedded down on green
branches the little birds in the treetops sang and bedded down on
the antipodes and bedded down on green stone the green grottos in
the deep woods the 1st violets were our bed the white
violets our bed it was in a green woods the 1st violets our
bed the little birds sang in the branches
+++++++++++++++++++++
the wild long bygone years you rest now under a cold
stone the little birds sing over your grave it is May 1 and
white violets the white violets blossom to your
feet you are 1 dead man the little birds in the treetops
sing on my heart lies 1 stone the cold stone I
sleep on the little birds sing in the woods

22.4.11

closed-up lilies like water snakes in water fountains May
bells namely = lilies of the valley (<u>Eng.</u>) exhale their
heart little notebook with blue cover : forget-me-not flowers
of the heavens slumber held me long today in its thrall the thistle
and rosehead in my dreams wafted tenderly your
shadow, we float through the lianas = BATHHOUSES of D.
our friend as with locks shaking his locks leads us into unknown
(branchlet) of tones ++++++++++
<u>in a trice &c.</u>
old tram ticket on parquet floor so siskin in thicket

23.4.11

oh you my green branchlet with your
sweet doublet like your white blossoms sprouted
out of my heart with this green
doublet oh you my sweet branchlet oh you my
green branchlet with your sweet doublet ....
like your white blossoms sprouted
out of my heart—the green doublet the green
dart of the season ....

"les études" in the heart the branchlets and lips of snow little petals
in my heart stag beetles fuchsias, I lied, don't want to eat anymore
don't want to drink anymore just want to go into the clouds, Marie,
I have raging winglets, Marie, I kiss you on each cheek, Marie, ach,
furor, Fauré, was in pain, was in tears, Marie, because my heart as
invisible as 1 monument, Robert Musil, ached and sniffled a bit
dreary &c., in the moment of awakening, Marie, with snow in my
hair and snow in my eyes ++++++++++ with blossoms, snow, back
then the branchlets of the cherry tree feeling their way through the
open window, nights, partridge and heather and on the paths, the
tears, on the paths the tears while the birdlets on their blue spoors
how I feel around for their hearts, and how I press them to my heart,
fuchsias for miles and miles of fuchsias, Marie, at your lip, Marie,
you whistle bird, Marie, wings, ferns, Marie, morning-waft of April
ach rosé, 1 little bit ach Fauré, dash holy water on lily of the valley
bouquets, Marie, and all things must be subservient, Marie (and
became a 6-sided face from it ++++++++++), Marie

28.4.11

30

and protégée LAPIN and I make
a big ear-shell with my hand
so that I might better understand what
you're whispering, then
my ear goes on
tiptoes and cries

as I awoke, lying on my back with my hands balled into sm. fists
and 1 adventure when we had long forgotten each other namely
the ribs of each little leaf ("études") namely we ADORED each
other &c. .... namely burying myself in the damp pillow, the
precise poetry of Ilse Aichinger, at the Markusplatz back then : head
to head, pigeon to pigeon : everything gray, Gertrude Stein. Carotid
artery clogged 1 dark summer—from the kitchen window thin fox
tracking the grounds of Wertheimstein Park, scrolling text, poem,
lamentations, deep grotto at dawn "études" scales, gender : 1 spider.
1 notion it was, in the middle of the night that 1 buzzing : fly or wasp
in the sleeping compartment but then, the humming went out,
cotton, falling back asleep .... on the RACK half-moon in bright
night &c., on the RACK 1 kitchen towel or flag, feelings frightened,
little leaves on the mimosa limp, and protégée LAPIN / rabbit, it
surrounds me 1 violet, PLUMAGE (Fr.), oh you white-flocked
cloud-bird—the ruching the rouge of the roses, the ruching of rain,
the fragrant mantles "Bataille"

3.5.11

"études" early vernal decay deforested chestnut
branches in grass sweet grass sticky chestnut buds while
sm. shako made of folded newspaper, <u>The Horae by Schiller</u>
1 dark voice
sounds from the back of the car, The Horae by Schiller, moon
and stars silver stitched = embroidered and back then Mama
her HANDKERCHIEF <u>stuffed</u> into her decolleté namely recollection
of 1 stuffing of handkerchief stitched with sun and moon &c. into
her cleavage : "ivy monograms" Jean Genet, a sort of niche
so she wouldn't misplace it mislay it, ach 1 stitched
snuffed into her bosom snuffed handkerchief so she always had it
to hand &c. alias Virgin of Mercy .... the
night sky stitched with sun and moon = embroidered, early vernal
decay in the glass underbrush in the flowerpot &c., after-
glows sinking in cities handheld fans of rosée oleander flower, death
carrying a torch the eye of the pansy sewn up .... <u>cunning</u>
<u>girls oh mock-orange   oh</u>
<u>protégée</u>

for C.F.
3.5.11

this branchlet of piano practice ("étude") branchlet practice
     ("étude") and
how M. Th. K. rushed on ahead through the darkness of campus
     namely at night
that time at night once again not wanting to be intruded upon the light
of morning <u>versus</u> the lark : locks in my eyes I mean the eye
shading shadowing with lark : locks (strands) of the nighttime
lark : locks <u>versus</u> the lily of the valley's bells sounding the morning
bells which I with darkened lark : locks darkening <u>versus</u>
the voice of my beloved echoing in my heart once more eye
of the beloved beckoning <u>versus</u> the lily of the valley's scent baring
shoulder and nape to me (whose glasses slipping to the floor with
a gust/little corner of the sideboard &c.) the pansy's kisses in the
     morning's
foliage <u>versus</u> the lilac's puffs of breath namely "the
lilac goes to my head .." &c., <u>versus</u> I sleep in the midst of re-
fuse/animals, rhetoric of the evening bells, in the springtime namely in
his CLOGS walks on I hear him walking in his wooden
pattens narcotic <u>florilegium versus</u> rainbow-opalescent
bolt ach death's blink of an eye <u>versus</u>
gullet : endlessly droning writings, *il tempo*, namely daisies time
<u>versus</u> in the light-blue kimono heavens white fluff fancy downy
     feather of
little cloud already disembodying .... am thunder-
struck oh murky mignonette green <u>versus</u> repeatedly I scamper at night
to the crucifixion glimpse colossal
facial features in the nighttime vestibule-mirror <u>versus</u>
puff of wind (mignon) &c., <u>sm. shako tatterlets of resignation</u>

5.5.11

emphasis, drama & feeling

(practice cahiers practice in the exercise books)
of as in of flowers nature or name "and dear ones
live nearby, languishing on the most isolated mountains," Hölderlin,
protégée namely I irrigated the loose plum tree. Littered
with Alpine roses (Mother's favorite), chamomile—sm. shako's
tatterlets of resignation, that is, mignonette : murky yellowish
    green of the morning
hush, the "ivy monograms," Jean Genet .... drove
death from bushes, laced-up snowshoes, found
breadcrumb in snowshoe—practice cahiers practice in the
    exercise books)
wafting études magnolias rain études, raindrop
kisses, thawing heavens, I want to walk in roaring gardens
burning gardens with you &c., NO death transfiguration perdition
no decease no goodbye no unison—ach lineament of
birch grove little white violet : practice cahiers practice in
    exercise books :
nightly death knell : slough : sm. standing water (photographed
by B. S.) sm. standing water deep grotto, behind tree trunks
barbed-wire roses switches lianas percussions, Her Highness's liver-
wort, after deep sleep this crying and imploring
forest island of blossoms and birds .... what
I did with the thorny underbrush .... here lilac blossoms
extinguished (in a gust of wind)

7.5.11

whereare all of these from the original diary entries or included also from the translator

34

namely the marmots the fairylike May I mean this fairylike spring in the paulownia tree ("on a Croatian plain .."), it always used to rip my heart out but now what does it matter, you know, what does it matter, "the Horae" by Schiller you know "I hunger for each of your lines, respectfully yours" while the Japanese cats, namely the cats weep actually waft : they wail you know what does it matter. Schiller's Horae, out of my mind I lie on my arms in the sun in the window, smelling the rain seeped for years into the frame, thin as a veil my sleep, rupturing toward morning, the wind namely this breezelet that blows in the nape of my neck (in the privet hedge) so fairylike May &c. brisk like back then in D. the wafting of May as we left the house and hand in hand and the pearls of dawn out of my mind I lie on my arms in the window smell all the rains seeped into the window's wooden frame .... as for the cat's eye-slits which in the ZONE = exclusion zone they wander around and weep and shriek / I mean the blue May : May practice "étude" ach birdlet practice "étude" at sundown &c., it sickles, the night, the claw of the music book, the knee-socks of the trees in the cemetery —ivy—such a dilapidated life, le kitsch, sm. folded letter in the WC .... "so it just came over me, last night up there, on a summit" .... Thomas Kling

12.5.11

twitching of the eyelids Beloved of the birdlets open
bird bills skulls in the morning how mouthwatering, billing and
    cooing around
a blooming branch, on a trembling branch, in the breath
of May singing dreaming delicate claws I mean clawing, like
Valérie like the sash of springtide fragrant like Engl. roses : walking
in ashes .... _Turner, overdressed_ or
window pillow pasted in the midst of the Engl. roses' aghast
puff. Glowworm's spoor : a diamond
that night as you, kissing me .... laurel in your
garden ("_how high the moon_") it sickles, the night, that time as
the Danube kept flowing around your feet, how it blows, the pen-
nants of the ships floating over (little Christmas tree's summer)—
his shadow suddenly loomed on my left, startling me
"whither dost thou wander" &c. then heavening me :
    hugging me,
the long hair tied back, you know, out of politeness,
mignonette presumably / cuckoo skits a little of that scent the
ruching of intimacy &c., the bedstead, namely

for EvS
14.5.11

"and if one travels to the Rhine" (I regress) and if one travels
to the Rhine at these words on the phone meanwhile/forthwith tears
burst and if one travels to the Rhine in a trice meanwhile/forth-
with at these words on the phone tears burst and if one
travels to the Rhine the locks
of the Lorelei I kissed them (I regress) in a trice and
Heinrich Heine and if one travels to the Rhine 1 breezelet that is
Heinrich Heine the Lorelei I kissed
her locks (I regress) the breezelets blow in the trees the leaves
of the wreaths .... on the waters and if one travels
to the Rhine the tears flow, 1 wreath on her locks (I
regress) Heinrich Heine and if one travels to the Rhine the
breezes blow

for Susanne Becker
16.5.11

exercise of the summer : zenith : with bare feet, magnolia tree, while working on this book the idea of a <u>sm. exercise</u> persisted : étude of a blossoming branch, of a little leaf in my hand, a Swiss pine LINE by the unprepossessing Francis Ponge &c., back then from the living-room window Mother's head, she waved to me for a long time while I ran down the street turning back again and again to wave, she was already fragile but she smiled in this film &c.

these serene dust vessels in the lung in the spring these strawberries before the convenience store gleamed, namely the cut-open melons halved suns—the sleep-nudging pills taken 2 o'clock in the morning, pecking pigeons at our feet, we sat on the little wall, Naschmarkt "Bon appetit" so that we cried, pecking people too "Horae" too .... also puddles falling into which we fell and crying. Also crumbs bread crusts souvenir-bags at the Naschmarkt (kitchen philosophy and suchlike), and how they fell : fell off : the kitchen table the little spoons swiftly as swaddled babes back then, the spoons had faces drizzling honey, right—"OK" and laughing "OK" from the telephone (like bedstead, that time) and then in the dreams with the tatterlets featherlets brushing here and there and every tatterlet I slang &c., then light blue in the window, natures shifting : murkinesses : Handel's "Berenice" e.g., bitter oranges namely chirping ACH like the young birdlet in the budding trees whose sawn-off branches in heaps in the wafting grass and purple tones oh deepest girl ....

21.5.11

1 leaflet kingdom of heaven in the hand summer
exercise, inexhaustible night, aura of the morning, dreamed of Orient
-al oratory, ejaculate in little satchel—woe!
throaty smoking chest tea-rose in the glass yellow shedding its petals
.... (peeing "good morning") : hyper-poetic
the secret (excreta) code, sometimes like flowers like the fragrance of
     flowers lily
fragrance, fragrance of peonies Tischbein's *Goethe in the Roman*
     Campagna or
on the Loire, this mixture of fragrance and repellent smell wild
honey e.g. on the kitchen table the honey spills or that
time with Valérie on the terrace of the cafe as it began to pour
down rain &c. and we pattered fitfully pattered (bene-
dictions) as one sends children to bed .... bitter honey "le
weekend" 1 leaflet kingdom of heaven &c. I heard the swallows,
how they cheep, flock at night to the rivers of Babylon where
we sit down and weep, the deep grotto : hollow of our
kisses (German is 1 kiss to the world, wrote Goethe),
silver RIND of the night, Jesus's mischpoke ....
.... she had dreamed the fragrance of myrrh, azure, and lilac
heart

on the Loire. Blueweather, am in the wind

28.5.11

but love opened up in the woodlet, linden trees namely fragrant allées, fields of apostrophes whither the elisions, flat expanses of feral speech flesh I mean flat expanses of feral speech elements— meanwhile shivers from the young jasmine bush showering down : out of the sweet jasmine woods meanwhile the verb trying to hide &c., I mean it doesn't occupy its orthodox spot but rather atomizes somewhere in the middle of the sentence : lesson learned from Elke Erb &c., and even if it were during the descent, these faded (debauched) peonies in the glass which <u>flanking</u> = flocking while the linden blossoms showered down and into the sm. rain puddles I mean they look like white membranes namely little-petal exercises of the jasmine bush = "études" meanwhile AMANUENSIS Elke Erb very slender elite university dressed in black standing across from me with thin locks, wasn't she, in tender virility .... dreamed of a voyage into outer space but in fresh colors <u>1 aisle of red fruits</u>, the true lily of the valley the "ivy monogram" .... mignonette, I cried, I'm surrounded by: 1 violet (murmuring) dog-roses études of spring namely fragrant ruching cheek to cheek the rain's heart to heart, the fragrant halls of the woods, in their arms "Bataille" <u>protegée</u> with dog-roses chamomile and carnations, so 1 bed of roses and gladiolas (Genet), birdlet's practice chirping in early evening ("étude"), practice in the evening before the thunder-storm, in darkened boughs, ach cried myself to sleep, and then TURNER appeared in a dream, *"overdressed"*

3.6.11

always the yellowish <u>bush</u> (in the hair) thorns on meadow's marge, iris dog-roses clematis in leas, little stem of withering jasmine in the glass still fragrant I did shed tears where the deep grotto and I on a bench under nut trees little leaves of crepe paper <u>steaming soul 4 o'clock in the morning</u> the morning hours, lianas bound into a sheaf and lady's mantle +++++++++++ your voice echoing on the walls of the deep grotto, foxglove angelica your blazing ears (dahlia embassies / *made in heaven*) when I open the window mornings the scent of a violet bouquet wafts in .... namely Magritte : violet-tuff in place of girl's face +++++++++++ little cup of snow (roses). <u>on the Loire</u> .... with a cane or a staff in a river you trace GROOVES, the adornment of birds, right, the "Marriage of Venice to the Sea" &c.—oh with a staff you trace GROOVES through the water : silken rivet or river, you trace GROOVES through this rivulet, so I comb your hair with staff or comb : on the staff 1 leaflet still which the river will remove, &c., hands plunge into flash and blood—

(I saw you again at the Stockholm airport it was a Sunday in December and we fevered to each other, I wanted to go with him to 1 other city 1 other country, "le kitsch" &c.) Poet of THE WASTE LAND, in a trice, <u>one of his sm. Karlsruhes</u>, freeloader time overtakes us, little cup of snow, "blossoms ex-blossoms" : Ann Cotten .... "scrounging a little" in the rustling of leaves, ach tear-weaving, you plant the little trees in the blue of the sky, don't you, such a heterogeneous hand

10.6.11

excelsior = the sublime path, wasn't I wearing a babydoll dress.
To break down heaven (reticence) something about you, discre-
tion : right earlobe left ear : blazing/blubbering I cried—not want-
ing to talk anymore in social situations, not able to talk, reticence,
cold eyelashes .... wasn't I, as I was 1 child, with ice skates, and
Mother freezing behind the rink's edge casting protective glances
at me, etc., torn saddle : not daring to talk to anyone anymore, not
able to meet anybody, Arvo Pärt with angels' voices invoking the
holy ghost to entice by shouting, ach world of dust : these crumbs
of DUST BUNNIES in the bedstead ("this is 1 ambush" : from
poem to prose, no?) .... and hadn't we, as we began to love,
traded handwritings namely matched them, the capital "E," e.g.,
be-bushed/and forest thicket, and hadn't they, the great-aunts,
often spoken of "*lisière*"?

and feeling cold (it was 85 degrees), lying there feeling cold
because (too publicly whiskey) because it was all too spellbinding
what I was reading, not finding the ten seconds to cover myself, I
want to be free of my past, oh I refuse to speak to elucidate to give
instructions zweige = *branches* : to point with one's finger : there,
go there! because one won't/can't explain, because the words don't
come : they glide around because they're OBDURATE don't you
know, I mean one wishes everyone understood us without words,
one refuses : one is reticent
++++++++++ he'd asked, back then : is desire capitalized?
am not sociable, over and out

13.6.11
Pentecost Monday

on a winter morning in Rumi's nightgown the sweet goldfinch. On a stiff branch on a winter morning the sweet goldfinch, songless, the stiff leaf on its stiff branch, the birdlet. The stiff leaf : broken leaf bitten to pieces by frost .... from its plumage falls 1 drop of blood, to the ground, to the snow—

(T.S. Eliot, poet of THE WASTE LAND : thirsting for his verses, yellow bill of the winter bird, snug snow, it was still very early in the morning it was still very green, very green sky and snow, I had lost him, I had cried over him, after 11 years I had almost forgotten to : little bill, darling, hiding behind the woodlot (Schweizergarten) to pass water : yellowish heart in the hollow of snow &c., little bill, darling, his traces long in the snow .... sat then as a goldfinch on a brittle branch : branchlet and tailcoat)

AGONY

17.6.11

43

sitting before the door watching what's going on in the world with
a little bell in one's hand and watching what's going on before
the door and seeing who comes and goes and feeling lonely, with
a little bell in one's hand and saying hello : being said hello to, and
with eyes slashing

potential threats ??

30.6.11

Variations on 1 sere branchlet, after Hermann
Hesse's poem "The Creaking of a Broken Branch"

little mimosa tree in the bed ach the little mimosa tree in the
bed, the little mimosa tree has given up : fallen leaves broken
branchlets the disheveled voicelet little mimosa tree, ruffled. Opus
number 101 the sheet of music blares the treble clef strolls in the
woods, 1 bit of brush on the kitchen table, the mimosa tree has
given up, its thorns are HYPER, golden sun blanched, I was
intimately busy with wishing, the branchlets the leaflets tousled,
the excrement shaped like a dog, brush on the kitchen table, the
deep grotto of our nights (written by the Loire), drove death from
the bushes, nectar of flowers and <u>protegée</u>, fetish of albatross, or
in the sudden (blossom)snow of your hand, gullet of the deep grotto
dried out which was actually 1 scrap of crepe paper &c., 1 pair of
thorns, the little mimosa tree past its bloom, moon-stains on the lake,
1 sudden lightning bolt from a storm, "ivy monograms," Genet

7.7.11

Reliquaries : ach what 1 pomp (like liquid chocolate and how the fingertips still smell of it a long time afterward), ach what 1 exultation : 1 empty suitcase, e.g., in which one could pack lilacs, e.g., bouquets of lilacs, &c., or all of Mongolia, e.g., the atlas, the withering little mimosa tree, the scent of jasmine or 1 songbird, overseas, the exercises the études, the gods of crying, the tears of mine he kissed away, &c., the sister's sweet ears, the dawn (Aurora's walking tour), the kisses the boyfriend's many kisses, and how he held his arms out to me over the set table, the violets ah Magritte's violet-face of a woman, the garter, the arias of Maria Callas, the changing seasons, the flames of the heart in the 1st frenzy of love, the rumoring of the little bird that mistakenly flew into my room, the adieu, the long adieu e.g. at the end, the long adieu at the end of our lives namely "as heretofore the birches or the willows held one's gaze" (Elke Erb)

10.7.11

with folded hands, writes Yannis Ritsos, telephone number Anna J. next to it "it was 1 impulse" my phony scribblings my arctic scribblings in mid-July, locks in my eye ach clouds in my eye, little sparrow in summer leaves, green clouds on your tongue, we climb up the Nestroy path banderoles in the wind placing our feet daintily in the brushwood, the harp sounds of clothes hangers in the wind at the open window, wire clothes hangers at the open door— these verses that shiver like branchlets in wind, maybe you should go ahead with this music, I write to Mikael Vogel, brunette-plate in the sand. Abstract, I say, abstract branchlet—aforestormed in my lifetime, did I drink up sleep satiate myself with dreams / Yannis Ritsos in the morning, my consoler loneliness &c., 1 pas de deux I wake up on a damp pillow, the steaming rosemary bush has delicate thorns ach peacock feather in nook, the young birds WRITE POETRY when they start to sing (I have eaten ants, I have beautiful-weather depression), the Dutch master pinches the nipple of his lady .... inconsolable rose left shoulder he shows me the night-blooming cereus in his garden inconsolable branchlet études "études" : "le kitsch" the dreams seep into the morning moon and flee through the beloved's pine bloom, soup spoon on the wooden floor : maybe destroy the beauty a little so that 1 deeper beauty can blossom

17.7.11

did the little tree come back to life, on the breakfast table
in the kitchen did the little mimosa tree come back to life timidly 1
new shoot like a little hand held out to me did my tears
revive its leaves green ORNAMENT in my eyes did its roots
renew themselves &c., whereas outside the storm
whereas my heart stood up like a tree like the bushes on the hill, "étude"
exercise, of nature whereas the beloved's locks veil
my face so I can't see his loveliness whereas
the cuckoos in my chest : whereas I live by contrasts

20.7.11

(ach Israel the twilight ....
we are walking step by step the
gardens willows meadows forests the blue
iris before the gate the liverwort
in tears, my little bed in the ground :
this is 1 summer like no other ....)

inconsolable branchlet études, leaflet of the mimosa tree they too know evening and morning (= exhausted or exhilarated), one should talk to them touch them sprinkle them with tears evenings mornings ach song thrush <u>rushing recollection</u> in dense bushes &c. and they *were* <u>nested in the finest jewelry of the valley</u>/they were wrested from the finest jewelry of the valley when we gazed down into that valley's depths : our gazes down the valley, 1 vertigo seized us, that incessant wind from the east .... Pannonian piglet. Or with sparse locks the longing, "Waldszenen" Robert Schumann, sachet little branch abstract hairy paws or in the sudden blossomsnow of your hand namely smelled like wild grass the night wind smelled like wild herbs études/tatterlets of resignation /thorns of sheet music, work without opus number

23.7.11

.... am I raging. This sm. mosquito in the morning when this sm. mosquito takes wing in the morning one fingernail high over the breakfast table while the rain, then this sm. mosquito disappears its extremities intact &c., or is the gloomy morning 1 kingdom of heaven with mosquitoes and ants and bees in my room so that my tears burst from me so that my foot I mean my foot is wilting while my brother looks at me with such blue-gray eyes that I sink I sink down into his countenance while the études exercises "études" I mean I see this pair of eyes before me : periwinkle flowers at the edge of the woods these 2 blue blue-gray flower-eyes in my brother's countenance ach 1 rain-morning my foot is sick like my heart, then 1 swallow flies through the house my mother is long dead Cy Twombly's "Orpheus," wax crayon on canvas, rediscovered in a book bewildered am I raging in my hut, my language buried in a grass bush (rootlet)

for Nikolaus Brinskele
24.7.11

I did drive by woods and rivers but I did not
see them instead only now back home do I see them
through tears and their colors and how they call and how they
greet me/the green compeers and at the windowpane the red
butterflies or petals of a geranium, namely
on a dish : flowerhead of a pansy &c., ach
on the balcony the sudden storm, sugar-handiwork
        in the lush garden ....
"then without a sound or a word I am gone," Robert Walser the
        raspberry leaves
and radiant

_____

11.8.11

and as I awoke : <u>the Phoebus</u>, bare feet,

tears, did you see them, the pale day-moon the hollyhocks the

sunflowers the *daffodils* in the vase did you see them, the shadows

on Franziskanerplatz in the hot noon the beggar's hand

in front of the supermarket, did you hear it, the voice of the lost bird

at midnight, through endless breezes the fire's

sheaves, so in the morning I write you into uncertainty ach

the platonic friends .... in the end one says

nothing, suppressed screams of pain and rage over there the crowns

of the trees the nightingales the branchlets : chimeras of twittering

    dreams, 1

fern frond on the tiled floor 1 summer evening AZURE, speed

and Fontana when I looked up into the sky—striding

through the green flames of the woods, in the rain

    in a deep hood, inconsolable

wax Christmas tree, inverted : green tableau

(oh to have to plunge into the depths of the poppy field, in delirium's

clutches, &c.)

maybe Thomas Kling saluted "<u>the rose-soles that</u>

<u>are starting to glow</u> ...."

for Georg Kierdorf-Traut
20.8.11

on the same page???

am so AT ONE with you, Cora with torticollis and task lamps : the
sun the empty plastic bottle falls into the empty shoe the varix, and
ice crystals on the snowshoe in midsummer this lily-of-the-valley
scent at the window mornings I noticed in her little summer-
house how she was crossing off the days on her calendar, once the
day had reached its decline, namely once its decline the day had
reached the snow crystals, she crossed off the day in her summer-
house and I was there and I saw how she crossed it off as if it were
already the past passed away but it was just the day's decline, and
I wondered why she crossed off the day on her calendar since the
day had declined but was not yet gone but the day had not yet
passed &c., already she was crossing it off on her calendar and the
midsummer flowers turned to the setting sun and it was the blue
and pink florets of the midsummer flowers that turned toward the
sinking sun, etc., ach Phoebus, waning : came like 1 blue-and-pink
midsummer flower and fragrant and the pigeons at our feet and it
was (EPILOGUE and the flower bushes 1 conflagration 1 dormi-
tion while Phoebus .... behind the mountains 1 devastation and
1 teeming while the woods' deep flames

20.8.11

fear/worst that there could have been more

les fleur flying

and the flowers spring up in your eyes when you stand leaning against
the tree next to the house and the flowers spring up
in your eyes the ones that stud the slope the woods when you stand
next to the house, you let yourself be carried by the sight of the birds
in the morning when you let your eyes fly up to the mountains the
mountaintops
the clouds .... ach Phoebus sinking behind the tips of the mountains
this rosy evening rose-colored night there you sit before the gate
of your house and feel the breath of summer I know
your long life passes by you, crosses over you, while the
moonshine's pearls = gleam of tears "études" your memory's ex-
ercises &c.
(green ghost-plants : Picasso's *Woman* sitting on an ottoman
with green sash yellow mignonettes)

22.8.11

as if I had written you into uncertainty (Sloterdijk) and might better
understand what you're whispering my heart inflamed, mild night,
I trample branchlets, cherry pit on kitchen floor, night glimmers
dear friend 3 *motti* by Cioran : the human world has become so
UNFAMILIAR ach let us go into the trembling green twig-work
and how it aspires heavenward ½ past 3 in the morning my head 1
tennis ball so hard and dumb the leaflets are still sleeping ach my
little sourpuss! faltering REBEL am I (Felicitas, your swarm song)
.... "le kitsch" Phoebus slithers behind the mountains—and in
the sweet faraway lands, look! your haughty water raged while I
waited for a kind raven to bring me breakfast on 1 tray decorated
with branchlet pink night-blooming jasmine and tuberose (1 illicit
message from the moon) ach how Phoebus sinks through the
blowing curtains I think of my beloved who through wondrous
breezes I mean periwinkle and star violas deceived me into the
deep grotto made of deep crepe paper, and once again, the cross-
stitch of the young lilac, dark daubs of fir trees (the white agony
of Monteverdi's moonlight, he says) and I fell on my visage on
my vision

30.8.11

"étude" "étude"
1 birdlet 1 finchlet at the gate
and before it came in it started
twittering ("*Styria*" "*Styria*")
(the more rendingly howled the dogs
at the entrance to the grocery store ....
bleached blinded by low sun the new
MS. I pull the curtains closed so the low sun
won't touch my writing : no cloud no violet I pull
closed the curtains so the low sun won't
bleach the new A-MUSE-MENT ....)
didn't we rhapsodize nights under stars taking hold of
each other's hands and kissing while the wisteria, while the amaryllis
bushes .... oh HALIFAX as a child
with ice skates

2.9.11

brambles on a garden table brambles of pale stalks brambles on a garden table on a balcony across the way pale stalks on the garden table pale tears "le kitsch" the pale awning over the balcony, the little dog BELTED, the cherries oh in your mouth the sky sky-blue "le kitsch" "you are the world to me" sang Richard Tauber and Joseph Schmidt brambles on my worktable pale stalks and pale tears 1 dry leaf between the pages of a book 1 white peacock with crownlet photographed by Simone Kappeler mounting the steps of a steep staircase, step-by-step in a wedding dress ("le kitsch") .... oh I was wingèd with the Halifaxes, the carving of my dreams chivalrous wind *"le vent dans la plaine"* by Debussy, night shimmers dear friend ½ past 3 in the morning I am a rebel the little leaves are still sleeping ach my sourpuss .... I was so sweet on him back then, gave him 1 rum-and-Coke to drink which he promptly threw up he had blond eyelashes white tuberoses the last swallows flown away 1 ocelot in Almaty in January twenty-eleven

(the waterfall in the blustery mountains .... as a child, the Halifax)

3.9.11

you're a lovely young firebird you're a lovely young snipe chamo-
mile tea and honey oh, chamomile tea and little dog with wafting
    white
ears, stormbirds, afternoon. The waterfall in the blustery
    (mountains).
Claude Debussy : wind in the plains white bread-bag Levi's jeans,
    ach
in the dusk in the moonshine the loneliness of the back balcony :
    out of
my mind. That time when he kissed me, genius of the pianino that
time when he kissed me, droplets from his forehead, a little bouquet
of dew while the cloud-cantos, the blue jay's wet feather .... behind
sweet underbrush 1 moss-mantle 3 white pebbles 1 alpinum.My
imploring = little bird bill and rose-red 1 goldfinch
                paschal. pinx.
("I'm thinking," she said, after hearing about her sister's accident, etc.)

and crying deep in the abyss : deep grotto, his white tennis shoe still in
the living room, belonging to the dead foot, inconsolable branchlet/
exercises "études"

8.9.11

and Waltz King, he said (the flyer had come, thumb broken, 1 mysterious assistant), the beer glass with the black felt-tip pens next to the bed, I say, sometimes so that I dive with the APEX of my face into the privy's tiles, fell asleep/fall asleep there, I say, at night, in my riven age in my injury while the hand my strange hand, that time, reached through the hedge fence of a stranger's garden, to touch the peonies (in full bloom) I mean in my ragged fur like a mangy dog, &c., my love for old dogs, sitting on my dirty cushion nights in tears what a vast bed of tulips, that time in Rotterdam, purple tulips, I stood still, yes, erect before them, this enormous regiment, such a tulip purple in her lush tusche, am demented dissonant obsequious while a restless star floods through me, keep dreaming of my dead friends keep dreaming of my dead friends, higher tractates, all of them with these bushes these waves these swallows, to see ach a good sleep

(oh how beautiful, were the mountains ....)

9.9.11

it was the meadow I walked through in summer
it was the beloved's hand touching my breast
it was the dance of the snowflakes my tongue stirred
it was the procession of years feeling the end
it was the snow blossom melting on my lips
it was the parents' goldfinches in the fir-forest range
it was the beloved's voice depths of a grotto green
it was the shine of his eyes like a flower's shine
it was the voice of the birdlet on the rose-slope
it was the waves of locks underneath the leaf-roof
it was late summer's chirping in deep midnight

bewildered am I, tuft of grass little rootlet moon as stalker
as the pigeon genuflecting in the grass—
I had to atone on hands and feet (o *Herr*)

14.9.11

was I sitting haphazard or happily on the bed did
the violets spring up on my grave did 1 crow come and squawk
at the window to jar me ("Mother is dead and
Sister is dead and the spring will come nevermore")
the moon sinketh and the stars sinketh oh
the waves of the sea. Letter torn rave and wreath
of smoke or what resounded, dreamed mignonettes on the
Loire "our lady of the voyage" namely I
was EMBUSHED whereas you stood at the verge
of the woods <u>and waving</u>

for Edith S.
26.9.11

you know endless infinity symbols in my
hand what does Ajax mean you know the sea ROLLS do you know
how the sea rolls up to your feet and over mountain
and valley your path and past the olive trees
wisteria woods bougainvillea you know the lianas
the lilies the waving cypresses and palm trees to the shores of
the sea you know you are alone (with pressure marks from love)

ach the dark clouds leaning on the window. Don't see any moon
any stars, but the rod blossomed in the sand .... for
our days are just 1 breath &c., for the water
rolling to your feet : bare feet dark blue the waves
roll up to you they take you in their arms so that
it is like 1 crying .... and I screwed up my courage &c.

(inconsolable branchlet you know, am dumbstruck)

for Edith S.
30.9.11

the cherries ach in your mouth <u>am your adagio</u> the pale
hair and pale tears. The carving of my dreams and
chivalrous wind the hollyhocks rosy on my cheeks back then
in the front garden of the house back then in D. back then the hollyhocks
    (mallows)
I was as tall as those hollyhocks (mallows) : blossom upon
blossom on the tall stalk—I drew up straight then I too
was as tall as those hollyhocks the sky sky-blue and deeper
wellsprings obsession and grotto .... oh see the beautiful
black angel flies over the sea to you its wings made of black locust
wood and <u>steadfast, the swans</u>

1.10.11

<u>inconsolable branchlet</u>

(1 homage to Alois Lichtsteiner and Tony Frey)

inconsolable branchlet, you know, am dumbstruck, this dainty heartache namely, music book's claw. I had slid down behind the mountains, my profile had changed .... 1 largo by Vivaldi the swallow namely flies through my parlor you say to S., you look like a freshly plucked cherry you look like a Flanders poppy you look like protégée, this beret isn't it so, and then we actually *were* sitting in Z.'s pub, late-afternoon sun breaking in, splendor of late-summer sun, everything in sunny cubes, wasn't it—the sm. dog and <u>frenzied the bushes</u> am EMBUSHED, from my fingers my feet my arms little alder leaves sprout and so I stand, green tree against blue firmament .... with rose-steps and with hereafter-steps your hand was flooding with blood, Antoni Tàpies and how he glowed at night, still violet-blue the night sky in October, and <u>protégée</u> : he gives it to his friends while they sleep, like Andy Warhol : 4 empty Coke bottles in the window ....

as he kissed me that time, 1 little bouquet of dew fell from his forehead onto my lip 1 little bouquet of dew, as he kissed me that time 1 little bouquet of dew fell from his forehead onto my lip : the day was hot and 1 hot afternoon, night shimmers dear friend, the waterfall in the blustery mountains, wild daffodils, 1 mountain that was called PIANINO, you know

1.10.11–4.10.11

in summer the flowered cushion we brought with us
in a bag, in the beer garden at the Rüdigerhof spent the afternoons
under the green baldachins of the trees such 1 summer in the back-
ground the shallow river and distant thundering of trains
and finches lovely in the branches the days in their sweetness in
the leafy heavens the languor of the heavenly bodies :
we listened, we kept quiet, we overflowed with the clouds

25.10.11

"Abendempfindung an Laura" the moon's rays have vanished the violets done blooming 1 white raven wants to bring me something to eat cried a lot and slept late the yellow star rose out of the clouds no one spoke to me I slept very late out there is 1 world that is strange to me but I wander in a world that is strange to me like loose leaves sweeping I have not seen my beloved in a long time I have not reached out my hand to him in a long time we have not kissed what has happened 1 broken light the violet done blooming the lost speech the loose leaves in a world come loose the mild LESSNESS the string of pearls of tears I want to see Giorgione the little ring shattered in Innsbruck in the mountains of Innsbruck, there the moon set and we walked over the mountains and there the stars rose and shone into the window ach the raspberry leaves in the lush garden "then without a sound or a word I am gone" ....

6.11.11

the repetition, and protégée of a blue landscape, in a dream, Jacques Derrida's long passages in Latin .... planted five kisses on my blue winter coat, and when I hear his voice in the morning the anemones bloom (le kitsch), our winter quarters! he would declare, as we entered the Sperl, as we exited the Sperl, as Valérie B. whirred up to us, the silvery eyes of the winter birds in the sycamore tree before her window had grafted themselves onto her beautiful face, &c., then suddenly she had this empathy to her features and I faltered, &c., bare little winter branch, I can already sense your early spring, I fling my arms around the neck of the human kingdom ....

the sun smokes, it is 1 winter-fire, the sun smokes, it is swimming in the cloud-sea

24.11.11

ach I barred my face with my hands while deep grotto, I had thought one thought all day, namely <u>little basket of kisses</u>. Snow and cherry blossoms as though I were in a Japanese early spring, tussock of affects, we already have a lot of memories in common, I say, heavy with sleep my goddess Memory, I say, Elke Erb calls me early in the morning and reads me her latest poem, while in the darkness friends call to each other out on the street, I watch the sidewalk so I don't fall, etc., fleeting dreams in the cafe 1 cigar-smoking man, doleful weather as the friend rides his bike through the city—the unforgettableness of Ann Cotten's ex-blossom, the décolleté of the daisies .... "in a certain sense we were fairly cynical," I mean that we alone, leaning on the window, my voice crestfallen &c., because the proximity of the friend freshly bleeding the wafting branches, namely loose leaves in a loose world or 1 blossom-amble : foolishly heavy with sleep in my goddess Memory, Christmas tree on the bedsheet

(<u>or is something afoot</u>, he asked, <u>1 quilt = 1 glory</u>) I was so deep in my morning dream that when I woke up I didn't recognize reality, kept seeing the last dream-image before me, namely Father with blindfold and SMALL MOUTH : tall handsome well-dressed (ach the silk tatters of dreams) .... it was all 1 bricolage

26.11.11

meanwhile garden-plateau namely from face to face, namely AT THE EDGE OF THE WOODS back then the clothes from my body he at the edge of the woods we stopped before the woods and he tore the clothes from my body &c. and shouted "cost what it may" .... the dark maw of the woods opened, I shed tears, tearing the dress the clothes the shielding rose, this deceit with which I come to my fellow humans day after day (withered white lisianthus and nocturnes), we look in at Miles Smiles &c., before I left on 1 journey Mother made the sign of the cross over me and I felt protected, then I came home and she expected a report on the trip, but I had nothing to tell, because the contexts—and in the evenings she'd sprinkle salt on my head to banish the evil eye, Jacques Derrida, this eternally bleeding wound this stigmata in the heart that the grown son no longer the tiny boy I once pressed to my heart and kissed : longingly—

(that I was fomented that I was flooded oh how beautiful, were the mountains)

28.11.11

in every nook and cranny I am sick in every nook and cranny I am
wretched the flitting films in my head : Boston e.g. '72 as we walked
down the avenue to get breakfast swarms of grackles winter '72
winter, my lovely, suddenly, on bar stools that time '72 in Boston,
suddenly, to get breakfast, on the avenue suddenly swarms of
grackles—then back to the hotel, coins in my coat pockets and I
repeated his declaration "the most European of all cities" (the
glittering films in my head = remembered this and that) "*winter,
my lovely*" we walked down the avenue to get breakfast at
the SALOON, that time in Boston, and then, once home, kept
repeating "most European of all cities," didn't I .... little music
book with pink cover weighted down with Cretan stone, which
she licked. These tears in the morning so much remembering
you know the oncoming winter swarms of grackles, of hearts,
kissed the top of my head gathered me onto his lap (Job, I believe)
while outside the swarms of grackles, the branchlets in which once
again red juices Pascal's *Pensées* miracle of the holy thorn &c.,
I covered my face with my hands so that I almost gave up the
ghost : on the Wienzeile the trash the tears : the entirety of my
writings 1 BRICOLAGE, the twilight of the ski-breast .... while
in the snow sunken flowers while finches in the bushes loveliest
while I am playful : playing with little Death

4.12.11

<u>loveliest</u> this little mouse's
tail sticking out from behind the wardrobe
not stirring . . . "To
a Mouse" by Robert Burns ....
I can imagine what you meant
but it was 1 thread string
cord .... (<u>cloaked</u>
early spring ach the tulips this
enormous regiment)

also mignonette verses of ruching in the hinterlands I hold my hands
in front of my face but the thousand years of tears slowly my
steps in the paradises of dreams little branch and wind rushing
of the Traun, blossoms ex-blossoms Ann Cotten but the wild
feelings find no words .... while the finches most beloved
in rosé you know in bushes with riven blossoms in D., &c.,
the hollyhock wends its way on its knees .... one morning I fell out
of bed <u>from sheer dreaming</u> back then the automobiles
had 1 running board you could sit on, 1 photograph
of my mother in which she is sitting legs crossed
in her little checked dress on the running board of the Talbot (foot-
note) I mean brunette hairdo (I write proëms) I
mean NOSTALGIA <u>with rolled-up sleeves</u> of December 2011,
unfolded his pinions, ach veiled moon in post-
surrealism, after deep sleep what a mute world : no letter from
friends, miracle of the holy thorn &c. while the song of the bird
in a faraway spring that is perhaps no more I am
HALIFAX am carrion my language buried in a <u>grass bush</u> while
the finches most LOVELY in the bushes
(<u>obsequious bow : I curtsy 1 little bit—the tempest gasps in the parlor</u>)

for Daniel Spoerri
8.12.11

these empire cats : gentian grasses (no moon) : now I go every evening oh late in the evening I go by the light I see it out of the corner of my eye I go past the light in the basement while the nocturnes <u>on the gramophone</u> .... CAHIER. Or in the Garden of Love's Sleep : I originated in expectorate, those were my hands and feet the flowers of my eyes the mirror of my brain grass-bushes my ears I remember Grandmother in Rubenspark lifted me onto a bench and <u>fluttered</u> my hand to her cheek (like a waltz) while Grandfather took me onto his lap and played his concertina, that's how I grew up. Don't ask me about the darkenings siblings of a flame fragmentary short bios had little consciousness the tender flowers in the garden (like so!) ate me up, I renounced worldly life bethought myself (at last) of my youth, etc., of my oboe d'amore. Whereas the anemones in Mother's arms, <u>it all depends on the prepositions</u> while I with hen with dove with sparrow on my head .... ach fuming swallow while the nocturnes in the flaming privet hedge lipstick on your cheek dear Prof. Beck : 1 inexact apparition were you, 1 sort of half-length portrait = film still variegated me I hadn't recognized you : without white coat, with tall hat, your voice from a great distance but you saw me straight off CREEPING up the steep stairs .... with alder leaflets in her arms my mother, perhaps 1 flourish am I, rotten am I, and ridiculous ah EMBUSHED 1 whirl in your eyes

<u>I'm crying : : : it's so glittery like little Christmas trees sparkling in the starry sky, okay</u>

12.12.11

I see a violaceous color on my bed see bouquets of violets
on my bed maybe throstle or dossier in the ob-
livion of a snowfall .... your clever eye and bouquet
of violets in December your clever eye and blond hair 1 crying
at the sea, that time, at the green sea of language and topos = temperance
(for Michi M.)

19.12.11–20.12.11

"to honeycomb" and to roam and to ramble with bare knees and grass and springtime meadow and spring and grasshoppers and March but today little Christmas tree, packed up, carried back home festooned with SOUTHERLY WIND and luck and little bells and suddenly you have blond hair ach my little birdlet let me give you a hug this is how the *SEASONS* go by and go past (in the wool store they also have honey my little beekeeper I saw her left cheek <u>crinkled</u> while the evening star &c. .... 1 star in formaldehyde 1 soul in formaldehyde 1 fist of liverwort then back then up the hill the 1st violet buried in my brain buried in the soil and white violets while the diapers the death poultices I mean she with the blond braidlet on death's acre with indomitable little teeth while at the bus stop the friend with wafting white hair but he did not see me although I called out his name, I mean in the sumptuous clover : is it 1 eagle so bleeds the deer, &c., dear rhubarb diaper .... cahiers, or in the Garden of Love's Sleep after Adolf Wölfli while the GALA ANGEL

despairing in this tiny (I mean disparagement) this tiny life all too short so it gushed out of your blue eyes out of your amethysts, avid vocabulary namely ferns over the stair-steps lace train of words long ago as he kissed me in oblivion snow, twelfth night and dying white rose. I mean, the duplicity of scents ....

(now she goes and stashes away the domestic bliss, &c.)

20.12.11

74

> "when I walk early in the garden
> in my hat so green,
> my 1st thought is, whatever
> is my Beloved doing? ...."
> Robert Schumann

Tinsel your hair ach your silvery hair went to sleep in your heart, lark on a tree across the way holy lark vaults into the air step-by-step in the snow-morning did you see, did you see me, you put your arms around me I was BE=MUSED I put my arms around the little Christmas tree or was BE=DEVILED bit of signal or *sentiment* in your eyes: bit inconsolable like tinsel your hair you trip in twigs bit of cloud you trip in clouds that time on the Opernring &c., at night, the inn of tears in the clouds then in the window the moon, then I think "you float aloft to him in the final hour" : darkened death flaneur of tears : house for hull little skull little bird bill lipstick after Walter Pichler .... I began, sputum, the sweetest tears, namely heart of quince ach you my quince-heart dearest rhubarb woodlet, storming on Christmas, then tears clouded my gaze (melancholic, CAHIER, or in the Garden of Love's Sleep, Adolf Wölfli, in the blackthorn) : spinning, psychotically susurrating on the Wienzeile where we in green bushes, I mean in the lungwort = PAIN-KILLER, all the books one has begun, namely *"Flädr Maus"* or "the fucking is done with the nether regions" (Adolf Wölfli) .... I saw the fields of lilies in summer and there you stood : 1 inexact half-length portrait in violet foliage while on the bedsheet 1 Cy Twombly tableau. And parting over the telephone, said "wei-wei" instead of "bye-bye"

(this insufficiency)

for Alexandra Strohmaier and
Christof Degen
22.12.11

bit damp and today, 28.12.2011 felt too inhibited to rinse, I say, bare shoulder of night-camisole, perennial feelings of dread about my age, I say, <u>day trip</u>, that time to the Vienna Woods, climbed knoll uphill steep feelings for KK back then, light of foot (was she = Silvie Fasching, when I saw her again after a long time, I whispered my age into her ear, then she whispered hers into mine, her reddishly shimmering hair &c. through the great coffeehouse window we were sitting next to : WINTRY, something like the fragrance of violets or sthg. similar, you're object-oriented, she said, pleasure-resistant, she said.) <u>Exercise in exercise books</u>, cahiers. Chamber of the heart : hiding in my heart chamber because I feel snug here (against the Ice Age), want to experience *sweet April* 1 x more, I say, breathing hosts of blossoms budding chestnuts = wistfulness, fleeing flora flitting fauna : violet birdlet in gardens .... I'm not interested in this "hereafter" that e.g. Christa Wolf in the moment of death before her fiery eyes, I mean. Schlingensief namely said the "hereafter" can't be so great that I, &c. <u>You deal with me</u>, I say, deferentially, HEAVENLY, I say, that I make 1 instrument out of my "I" or sthg. similar, so I brush alongside my feelings as with snowflakes, don't I, and alongside these films in my head : DISASTERS—(while the bird's song after a distant spring that is perhaps no more, while the finches most lovely, you know, in bushes with riven veins and mallow kisses in rosé, &c.), meanwhile he had mistranslated "unlit" .... am sick or at least stricken so that I (wretched) sitting on Franziskanerplatz in the shadow of the Franciscan church .... <u>and trembling</u> .... tattered sleep heating gone out, GRAMO plays "Abendempfindung an Laura"   *she* really studied something, in the Wiental, I was so dumbfounded I say, while you, over the Stubenring, aflutter

28.12.11

76

ach my quince-heart,
did you see the sm. swallow on the last day of the year did you
hear the bird's song on the last day of the year namely it was the
GRAMO playing the bird's song, e.g., sm. swallow as we in the
cornflower-blue sky .... NOTEBOOK = CAHIER the
teardrop streams in the fiery garden namely the bird's song in a
distant spring that is perhaps no more &c., deep grotto in the after-
glow LAPIN = RABBIT these verses quivering in the wind my
foot is withering in a grass-bush wet bird-feathers namely on the
last day of the year, and once more

31.12.11

Marcel Beyer says DELICIOUS!, we're driving through Cologne eating tortes, it's Carnival, I remember, I think of Robert Schumann ("Carnaval"), it must have been 25 years ago, later he moved to Dresden, the branches were already burgeoning. He drove a 2CV, wrote poems. End of January the 1st blackbird. Then eventually the feeling of horror at one's own end, for instance, at ¼ to 3 in the morning this was composed. I caress my father's brow, the deep-blue sweetly fragrant hyacinths in the glass, I mean this <u>leafy</u> : kinetic measuring instrument that keeps moving on the white page namely again and again a jolt back to the left margin of the notebook (CAHIER)

3.1.12

like my rose-red ENTREATY like my little bird bill I mean my
little snipe : those aren't rays that the sun—I mean <u>puffs</u> over the
water those are white cloths : like the ones Jacques Derrida recalls
when he thinks of his mother's "*periods*" namely thinks of the
"branded" cloths of her periods, namely the sun as his mother's
BIDET in the bathroom, etc., there she would leave <u>her cloths</u>
LYING AROUND .... <u>lipstick</u>. Like the winter bird that plum-
mets down, namely such Pisa strokes = suns banderoles where the
leafy siblings at the beach I mean crouched, ach the ribbons that
haunted me where the sun plunged into the waves ....

3.1.12

Kisses little Man Ray's ach the lilac (lovely) hyacinths in the glass fragrant myrtles like lilac-hued spring already in January = winter aconite you put forth lilac blossoms, whereas .... walked up the footbridge while little sister was already waving to me from the window : expecting me, back then, I carried cahiers close to my heart waved back <u>whereas, amid the thorns</u> whereas the blurred moon would pull the plastic clouds on strings across the black sky I mean <u>1 freak</u> namely cataract of tears and dreams, cookies or biscuits : this whole sm. world, I say, in the rear-view mirror of the dressing room my back's astute skin, kisses, little Man Ray's, <u>whereas amid the thorns</u>

6.1.12

certainly ceremonious : in thicket and thistle-holt dreamed of the Madonna with the flower fan namely as I opened my eyes this morning .... in her arms she held the dream vision of the Madonna with the flower fan (<u>potpourri of pills at night</u> &c.) and when she asked me my age I froze, namely the lace train of fright glided over my confession .... incantation that dragged on through the next days and nights so that I felt no pleasure = delight in the <u>eye of language</u>, JD, on this flower fan while I leaned on this flower window crying and pulled the lace train of dreams through my CAHIERS writings also aussi <u>sites of the flowering plant</u> .... that time in Rome aussi, 1 week before her decease passed by the garden of the Hotel Lord Byron where the little lemon trees with their yellow fruits I mean <u>if she were to die</u>. The salt from sweat in the palm of her hand, 1 trauma because I had revealed my age, and cried because I could hear it rushing in my ear : 1 waterfall in the mountains in my ear like that time with the twins Egon and Guido (we) skipped and ran alongside the wayside of the tumultuous brook

12.1.12

"<u>languished</u> almost the whole day with
BUBI in the garden and
find flowers and blindworms,
<u>festive</u> in thicket, thistle-holt
........"

and everyone asks what are you reading these days &c., while the
little skull = little bird bill (*boxes*) on the doormat : <u>potpourri of</u>
pills at night &c., <u>aussi the dying</u> dark-blue hyacinth in the glass,
1 library for you and back then the grass that grew in the gardens
of D. aussi the gruesome films in my head, '54 in Salzburg as I set
off for London, 1 vehement spring, we found 1 hotel room to say
goodbye but my memories have been erased, don't remember
what happened there in that hotel room, I didn't want, you know,
I did not want to go away at all, didn't want to leave you, on the
wall 1 (melancholy) oilcloth bag but I wasn't crying about that,
JD, when will I turn into 1 swallow

all just bricolage. Rolled up in a ball the dirty laundry on the piano
&c., WHICH DID ME SWEET, oh I wandered, lost, while the
leas in leaf : this forsakenness of my eyes .... <u>looking forward</u>
<u>to angel-living</u>

12.1.12

upon looking at Liesl Ujvary's photographs "Zwentendorf Nuclear Power Station" and discerning a shadow, or the smell of burnt hair, I say, the white garments namely safety suits swinging from the ceiling actually <u>turning cartwheels</u> through the protected area, like ghosts. Behind them, colorful languages and lockers, little iron baskets, hoods, clothes, the beauty of the red elevator doors, the goblets of the steel tulips

("a murmuring in the pit of my stomach after consuming .... an apple, e.g.")

14.1.12

1 upheaval in blue and green as the five-year-old son's
dearest wish : <u>to go flower-picking with Mother in
the meadow</u> : was granted
(then clapped his hands to his face, started to cry)

for Günter Roitner
15.1.12

after the death of the mother the deep feelings belonged more
profoundly to her since the words SOUL and TEARS rose on her face
ach shattered, her eye and mouth

17.1.12

these tears namely these tears fall glittering from the heavens my
tears plummet glittering from the heavens namely thoughts on a
<u>bewildered</u> bird image by Ulrich Tarlatt .... Dürer's violet
bouquet and fresh flowers and blindworms <u>ceremonious</u> in thicket
and thistle-hair I mean *Styria* : hiked through the MYSTYRIAN
Alps while early spring's tree crowns droning in an undertone,
angel floats in its enclosure, "I've been on the moon," she says.
"Were there other people?" I ask. "No, just me," &c. Sites of the
flowering plant (<u>ach if she were to die</u>) and placed the heel of her
hand on her lip as though to ruminate : LIONHEARTED, and
learn Jean Genet *by heart*, but that's not what I'm crying about (at
¼ to 3 in the morning <u>this</u> was composed, when will I turn into 1
swallow, the blue sweetly scented hyacinths in the glass while we
<u>aflutter</u> in Rohrmoos over the alpine floor, &c.)

19.1.12

<u>A message of greeting, e.g.</u>:

I mean I am a constructivist am an imaginary invalid brought 1
teardrop little Christmas tree home although CHRISTMAS is
over. The little son plunged one of my curly hairs plunged one of
my curly hairs into his pants pocket, blackbird at my side I had a
teardrop in my eye and fur, then looked to the side : what a poetic
idea &c., then played "Abendempfindung an Laura" again, ach,
you're all like 1 open book, <u>I am spellbound in your midst</u>

22.1.12

<u>that's how he teased me, on the picture-postcard</u>

.... dreamed there was 1 Jesus sitting in the classroom, I *was* 1 teacher, after all, maybe it was clematis—composed this at ½ past 3 in the morning .... 1 snow fell and he fell in the snow like 1 child (<u>sat over books of the most recent Assisi</u>). As for the mother's WEDDING RING she rang with it against the water pitcher on Christmas Eve so that it sounded like sweet silver bells to the child, who started to cry, &c., namely before the moon, little doves cincturing the angel, and so I wonder did JD's mother use those little doves to stanch her monthly blood?

barred my face with my fingers so that no one would see it : its unfathomable ugliness .... the sun did actually circulate in the bay of angels over and under the swimmers <u>moon membrane</u>, in Nice

night practice = étude : Rhode Island, '71, in Rhode Island to bed that time America '71, at his side, I say, exhausted into the CAHIER (Dürer's violet bouquet over the bed &c.)

(to give away everything save
the last shirt)

22.1.12

"my motherlet mozambique-let my
motherlet violet-pale" : I wrote
in early summer '65

1 Manet : <u>female nude with white rubber gloves</u> .... I mean
the poem that I wanted to write tomorrow I wrote
yesterday. Thin as a veil the sleep of morning so easily
torn, dreams bitten in two, I say, from the GRAMO
    (sweet dreams, I say, their sentiments. Sweet
    pavanes their sentiments. Sweet dance steps of a
    dream which converge with the waking state, e.g. :
    I open the wardrobe to look for something and the fact
    that I find the object immediately fills me with glee /
    sealant feelings)
Ravages of a dream as if in a waking state .... had 1 port-wine
stain on my forehead at a tender young age : had the shape
of a continent, had 1 Africa on my forehead that faded
with the years—namely the girl with bangs
    "Thanks for the blackbird photo which I already love :
        devoured
    worm looked to the side, teardrop in fur .... <u>oh</u>
    <u>if she were to die</u>"

for Edith Schreiber
23.1.12–24.1.12

these paws these painful paws that is stiff ankle joints staff
or crutch in each hand but in the dream, "a brisk pace." In Italy
flowers, years ago in Rome swelling wisteria, and cats, someone
took a photograph : in a TRENCH COAT : of me, I still remem-
ber the corner : the street corner : would still recognize it some-
where in the slums &c., famished cats .... past the Hotel Lord
Byron the young lemon trees in the garden : squeezed tears from
me—unforgettable years : the glittering sea seen from the train :
<u>pieces of sea</u> azure-hued pieces of blue seen from the train, a trip
to Jesolo : VELLEITY, I say, le kitsch? and thought-pictures, tear-
stained and the most sumptuous clover, Adolf Wölfli's bright eye-
tears, lucky clover and clover-leaf *shamrock*, cloven excrement in
the bowl .... ("I have been on the moon" "Were there other
people?" "No, just me"), flotilla of winter birds over the roof, bird
by Ulrich Tarlatt, woodcut, with long sharp bill, <u>such 1 blow</u> &c.
then rang Mother supposedly rang the doorbell, études and cahier,
and because Wally could look over from his gravesite to the urn-
grave of OUR DEAR MAMA who'd just been cremated ("Mama's
burning") Wally could send over <u>an arrow</u> to the urn of OUR
DEAR MAMA I mean <u>arrowing</u> and because they could see, could
look over at each other : Wally at MAMA and MAMA at Wally
(<u>who at age 15</u>). So might I manage the exercise = étude today
thanks to the diligence of light, &c., lost glory = *verlorene Glorie*,
twisted yarn of the hawthorn bush while the coil from the <u>gramo</u>
rolled into the meadow, oh that I was once 1 stripling and crowns
of wind and sea wove round my brow .... 1 trotting at his side,
<u>at night</u>, and in the end they say it was at my cheek that he died

28.1.12

ach I had had 1 telephone (beloved) : had
snow-stars = étoiles sparkled in the tender
night as Lenchen led me .... home

Tàpies dead, he. Had me fooled or whispering from the little gar-
den, his bare foot like the bare foot in the Fra Angelico in a
meadow that was 1 bit sloped &c. with tender blossoms = étoiles,
midst the sea. Millefleurs detail of a painting by Fra Angelico, oh
we sank into the cabbage whites, sank down into the cabbage
whites as haunting pensées .... I thought 1 Debussy : no, said
Susanne B., 1 Haydn : ach it devoured me while feverishly strewn
butterflies, insatiable little caplets, wasn't it so, étoiles, star-
sparkling in the heavens, I mean I wake up with the blisses of ....
I mean my grasp, the mountains are within my grasp, when the
mountains on the horizon are within my grasp, 1 rain comes.
Maybe I have become somewhat proud of late, I say, and so I pray
all the more, kneeling or standing, I say, according to JD, it was
dissimulated, I say, the raw singer circa, one evening, étoile, said
Traudl B., she felt lonely, which aggrieved her, and so she crept
into 1 bush to answer the call, now we are alone, she said. With so
many flowers and ornaments, the Virgin Mary drawing nigh

(ach little heart ran riot with fear circa many years ago, deep-black
blueberries, how they grew wild in the woods, or SNACKING on
the wood-beauties namely infiltration of a love

7.2.12

just DRIFTING OFF for days : then suddenly the outburst : little girl, snow, all these dainty ants that teem = labor for us, this daily baker e.g., and then I dipped my shock of hair into the full honey jar and <u>stiffened</u> with eclecticism, etc., very agitated dreams, hybrids, in tears at times, in dreams : <u>soul</u> that bursts forth from the eyes, I say, I couldn't believe. Star-speech "étoile" while <u>aeroplane</u> of the night like zooming humming insect or instinct 3 o'clock in the morning through the night (behind curtains), I did not know him but he entered the stage as an angel with disheveled curls especially at his nape as once the beloved had had little curls at his nape and I <u>cut</u> cut them off with a LITTLE KNIFE while he slept .... even the dying hyacinths were still fragrant, though it was circa the scent of putrescence &c. 1 secret : étoile or fleur maybe also PARKINSON, finally just asked him his name, he led me from the murky upper floor across the Mozart stage to the elevator cabin, on his cap pharaoh-roses .... back then I had a haircut *à la garçonne* (in God's hands now), and as he <u>wondered</u> into the little heart I fell under his spell, I mean, he found the haircut's heart shape at the nape wonderful

pretended to myself that I was READING but I just dreamed it namely with bare feet over snow-roses realms such a cold vow

10.2.12

"oh I hold you so close .... what
Eng. lady-tatters, FM, such lovely
lady-tatters, FM, namely creeping up
the Wollzeile held out a few coins
to him, man selling the AUGUSTIN, then
heard him DECLAIM to me,
probably Russian prayer &c., sitting
on a stool before the large mirror in
the AIDA cafe chain .... what lovely lady-
tatters, creeping up the zippered Wollzeile,"

ach little girl, snow, &c.

So 1 motto on a Sunday morning, you say, so 1 motto upper right
on the empty page, plural *motti*, you know, the February-cold
EVISCERATES you I mean rips your soul right out of your body,
doesn't it, while the February sun drills into your eye in the rue
de Regard, you say, indeed, you say, the birthdays come much too
often, I mean, one resorts to chemicals &c., nerve-snow of the
most brazen myrtle-magic and protégée when in slumber the pen-
cil draws = scribbles 1 branchlet on the paper over and over,
falling to my knees oh Madonna! my language entombed in a
grass-bush in the snow-blanketed woods where we camp foot-to-
foot and finch most LOVELY in the bushes .... cooing gibberish,
ferns over the stair-steps, let us hold each other in the white sloe-
thorn = with our sloe-eyes, the good things learned dipping into
books most LOVELY (we divvied up the grub, didn't we, all com-
posed in loneliness, today ½ past 4 in the morning, "miracle of the
holy thorn" (Pascal))

for Erika Tunner
12.2.12

so gruesome from the GRAMO, *la neige* : it is stuck
in the heavens, oh the flower's EYNE hiding
in the snow ....

the swarm in the snow I was dreaming away dreamy swarm in snow dreaming bird hopping from branch to branch, pussy willow in February snow, blue-black locks of a <u>middle-aunt</u> : fell down out of her silk dress, fell into blossomsnow, 1 drop of blood on the parquet .... (that's how he teased me/picture-postcard), this tight textile, <u>and *lyrics*</u>. For the duration of the orgasm the soul really does leave the body, I fold my hands on sacred knee, *ach bleib bei mir Herr Jesu Christ*, you holy thorn, <u>whereas</u> the bird's song after a distant spring that is perhaps no more <u>whereas</u> the finches most LOVELY, you know, in bushes with riven veins, no disco living, let's hold each other in the white blackthorn, my darling ah my Agnus Dei and swishing, the bushes : delirium of a love, 1 buttercup dale, 1 buttercup death, *les étoiles* and mallow kisses most LOVELY, winter quarters in rosé, Café Sperl in the heart of the bird's flight he fulfills my every wish, we sit very cocooned and <u>discreet</u> .... Schlingensief writes, how great can the "hereafter" really be, I wouldn't want to leave this world for it .... all calculation all bricolage : I have no poet. ethics. I mean we missed it, <u>missed summers</u> flowing, flowing away, fanning out on the ramp of the ALBERTINA : the summer's fanning breeze, with eyes closed, Latin in his lap &c., wondered after waking what it was that had made me so glum the other day, this tight bodysuit, oh Madonna, was so unfathomably undulated, <u>something comes to me</u>

23.2.12

after 40 years (after waking) I see the nun shave my mound of
Venus before the operation, from the edge of the bed <u>the stone from
Crete</u> falls and thunders, <u>the stone from Crete</u>, 1 thunderbolt : <u>gift
from Crete</u>, I burst into tears, in Cattolica my ride on the back of
an elephant made of papier-mâché, the sky bleeds, out of the sweet-
ness of deep sleep the thunderbolt of <u>the Cretan stone</u> wakes me
and protégée, the mother teaches me how to pray, Mother's
brunette hair her blue pair of eyes, deep childhood = deep aquifer
forget-me-not and little thunderflower open my eyes and Father is
carving the willow pipe, golden mornings through the skylights,
the sleeping room ach, the summers of D., so breathes love between
you and me, decades rushing by, the afterglow intones the colossal,
coltsfoot leaves next to the stream oh do you remember we sat
down and tussled with them : toilet-leaves, the glow of stars in
August the cuckoo's cry, swallows take to the road, salamander in
evening sun, my farewell to the distant fir trees and on the slope
greens the vine .... Father cried often .... *nuage* the cloud I
have never understood the fates and what happened to me we
kissed and our hearts went up in flames, Renée put her arms
around me maybe she was 1 lilac bush and from the GRAMO
1 Bach cantata I dance the tango with Renée the tiny globes of the
dying mimosa, that is to say, Vichy, if I'm not completely mistaken,
here strict grackle <u>hidden meaning</u> the differing signatures over
the years, hysteria of the <u>morning vows</u> ....

<u>(and almost choked by all-too-knotweed)</u>

25.2.12

pleated grotto : 1 x I will
be so tired that I will only
want to sleep that is I will never
want to wake up again = with unlikely
heart I will then dream of my life
that is gone or I will dream of
how it might have been .... ach
I have wasted my life. Instead
of rapping my knuckles I cried
it away .... circa with my head on
my arms on my desk, &c.

the everyday the daily things I could always talk about with my
mother, I say, the soft collar on my pajama top cocooned me in 1
childlike way which did me good while she said, you are in 1 child-
like way thus assistance or grace .... such a horn of plenty lan-
guage in the early morning I mean I barred my face with my hands
so my thoughts could form more easily, it was like 1 ritual and she
was buried under flowers .... 1 thin piece of clothing feels like
the surprise of the onset of the earliest buds of an early spring
namely little branch in which the saps were mounting and which
had been working at it nights, to unfurl, I say, ... and am totally
enclosed inside my body and won't ever get out again &c.

(and they probably never did meet, ER and John Cage, namely
like cloth-of-gold, then they burst open in the meadow, with blue
eyes : violet and liverwort on the hills to Leopoldsberg, while the
blowing of the storm in early spring where
your eyes are roses (Jean Genet)

29.2.12

the sm. provender of his little body = she always spoke of his "little body" &c., leopard-skin &c., 1 snow and cherry blossom, 1 snow and bushes of white affects, we wanted to go to the movies. In frosty temperatures on bikes through the city and *lyrics* if I'm not completely mistaken, here a strict command : to never show these notebooks to anyone, and then we race past the flea market, 1 sm. piece of a hard roll from the previous day in my pocket, the beginning of the end of the grieving the provisions : am provided with longing for you (he teased me or whispering from the little garden), moon snowflakes, 1 throstle in the thornbush and it's Rosi, and when I said, "the ice-cream shop will soon be open again" you said "I remember that you say these words each spring, I mean, that we've loved each other so long ...." I say, do you remember who I was—*winter, my lovely* ach in all colors the cries, writes Derrida. In the midst of the beautiful moment = sleep, 1 bell-ringing : I think "nuage" or "fleur" or "neige" in a trice, and herringbones on your cheek, *winter, my lovely* while the little grass underneath the snow

7.3.12

where your eyes are roses = Jean Genet, the
soul-filaments 1 + 2, bedewed by the blue-
black torrents of the sun ....

during the slow walking in tears in the dream 1 vast feeling of hap-
piness for I had e.g. 1 blanket strapped around me while the presi-
dent of some western state was serving as a friendly waiter in an
inn, raw meat was offered, we declined, I smiled at circa 1 little white
dog at the feet of a lady also completely in white, I mean 1 series of
white dreams, 1 chalet whose roof was weighted down with boul-
ders how I cried, still dozing off 1 pressure in me to look at the next
day in the calendar, to consult, 1 feeling of happiness while listening
to Satie, when his sister-in-law died he sketched her shroud : trape-
zoid on the death notice HH told me last night over the phone ....
I felt weakened yesterday evening in some way, he bent over me
with white flowers and kissed my neck which I felt all over my body
and had to smile blissfully, it was 1 ONSLAUGHT and then she
whispered to me, at 66 he can no longer lie with me for 1 hour like
he used to, it's down to 5 minutes .... while drinking I almost
choked, felt my eyeballs bulge from their sockets and roll down
my face, it was 1 brushwood : 1 early spring : 1 descent into the
initiation into the pebble, after Francis Ponge, &c. ....

(if you cut 1 piece of cake into smaller pieces you can eat it for longer
than if you ate the whole piece at 1 x, if you swim on your back you
can see the heavens' rolled-out shawl, e.g. If you open your eyes
under water the fish of the sea will encircle you I mean the white
coral that looks skeletal in the greenery of the deeps, etc., and were
you to cloud over the sea you would hear the singing of the waves
like birdsong &c.

14.3.12

"the scream" like the open mouth after Munch, in the mirror, they have opened, the buds, and on the grass the sputum .... and how she spares the sm. flowers with her soft feet "Hanna" : want silver want moon don't want Phoebus don't want gold, from the GRAMO : Satie, "And I don't like the cool day. It has 1 glass eye" = Else Lasker-Schüler .... Tipp-ex on Hölderlin. Delectable the withering of the soul toward the finale, isn't it, I say, when I open my eyes, you know, like birdlets that looked : look't : tears namely in the blue CAHIER, &c., I am in receiving mode .... she said on the phone, on the little pail, in the morning, and for my other business I went down into the cellar and protégée nuage and neige, étude, étoile and cahier. It snowed on the TV screen my soul had left for 1 few hours, I say, this egg, I say, because I was walking up out of the parking garage and almost lost my right hand, how SATIE rips out my heart, &c., ach I lived here 1 x, as if I, in a Japanese early spring, sheer snow and cherry blossoms behind my eyes, raspberry-colored early evening, chique sm. Minervas, so Alexander Nitzberg, as baffling circa in tears, in the castle garden young deer budding chestnut branches sawn off in the grass, &c., while on the wayside picking 1 few flowers : tender commerce : the green parrots whirring in the streets of Buenos Aires, like Technicolor phlox or fetish (glittering), licked the sweat from his body, right?, to have done so. I saw the photo of a child, very BLURRY with inexact shock of hair 1 EDEN, 1 painting by Francis Bacon circa blurred, that's how my writing wanted to be, arrangement of the folds Ponge, at 1½ years old I lay in my buggy in a draft and got sick, and since then .... 1 honey dripping down onto the meadow namely this outbreak of feelings in 2 brains lying opposite each other, e.g., unconditional BEAUTY

17.3.12

over the wavy line of our "local" mountains from the window
over the rosary of our "local" mountains in the afterglow the sm.
balancing pole, the soul-threads 1 + 2, black-and-white doe hare at
the open door leaf : discovered the tennis shoe and the T-shirt one
atop the other, black-and-white, which brought tears : stream of
tears, white <u>little pail</u> covered with furred shoe : black-and-dissonant
whereas in the hollows of an ossified memory whereas familiar
memories lost in the deep (green) crepe-paper grotto of my con-
sciousness .... while we crowded, into the off side of a Naschmarkt
bar, I mean, where the bright sunlight couldn't reach : the young
hostess, the overwhelmed eyes of the young hostess so we stepped
back : took several steps back : we were not heading for the yellow-
green of the off side, I mean verses and mignonettes in the depths
of a Naschmarkt bar, have transitioned to a moderate collaging ....
while saying I did not want to enter a private apartment, she sat in
a little armchair in the still-bare garden (it was late February) while
in the neighbor's garden children were playing with a ball &c., ach
I sat in my bed half the night and looked for the sons and daughters
of the snow, "the site of half-sleep." How it steamed : what it boiled
down to what it depended on namely if certain words = word-
groups of reading matter had the power, in the eyes of the artist,
to metamorphose : into similar word-groups—that is, to regenerate
.... "<u>of the body from the time before the mirror</u>" : this Parisian
cafe that smelled like fish, not far from a fish stall, on the one hand,
and on the other : naked before the large mirror in a room at the
cultural institute in Paris early morning many years ago : and
already then the flaws of the aging body .... in the package
Turkish figs and atop them a large gray-green leaf = FIG LEAF,
1 gift from Isabel C., life-size Easter sponge cake lamb that could

stand, dyed eggs in a little basket (this one here I BOTCHED),
everything elliptical, I say, ach early spring, and we sat = sank into
the warm sunshine

19.3.12

saw a blackbird's head : teardrop in the
fur (worm in the hair part), <u>raw singer</u>
circa one evening and étoile : Traudl
B. that time and crept under 1 bush :
TUFT to answer the call (at
night), set to music, lip, the Virgin
Mary <u>draws nigh</u> .... did
snow-stars sparkle étoiles in
the tenderness of the night as he led
me   (home), ach did my heart
run riot with fear years ago
circa deep-black blueberries how they
the wildfire of the woods namely
<u>snacking the wood-beauty</u>

now we are alone, with so many flowers and <u>ornaments</u>, she said,
namely Satie who floats me away, blue-eyed the sky in the morning,
actually the blue curtains : the little pleated skirt at the window,
the little pail, he says, you're very symbiotic, such 1 luck that I was
in your arms, in my dream &c. <u>the CAHIERS are 1 book without
progression</u>, of crouching cowering and creeping <u>namely so that</u>,
I've read the book 3 x already .... Frank Zappa, roam around in
my abode waiting for hysteria for hyacinths for <u>loafers</u>, decades
later blue Danube the sm. aggression still in the classroom (in my
dream). Before the reader backs out because the air of reading has
become too thin, I offer him a morsel of intelligibility (I'm reading
haiku from the "Little Book of Complaints" and he led me through
the little garden that ran along a narrow path, here's the budding
apricot tree, he said, at night the tears tumbled, as the shadow in
the woods) .... I found the little INSEL volume with the haiku
in the bottom drawer of the tool cabinet, I say, the last time I met
Eleonore F. in Germany I saw her without actually taking her in,

full moon in the sky ach sprouting herbs and grasses whereas the
rupturing blossoms and the mountain cuckoo's calls .... 1 long
path from THINKING OF YOU AND WRITING TO YOU, I
say, and enclose 1 tear in a letter to you I mean eggshells in nests,
snow-roses, do set your sights, Madame, on the buds of the apricot
tree, he said, circa violets, liverwort in the depths of the garden

23.3.12

"we didn't find anything *last minute* ...." as if I were gasping for breath one last time, I have grown lonely, in these gusts of wind, heart caterwauling, are you reading my mind via my eyes, I say, with Fellini on the freshly swept grounds of the Naschmarkt, I could always read in his visage = a vision and while I was reading my eyes closed, cried, like the sky, contracted, 1 parchment and while the sky kept darkening with dusk .... I'm 1 person without empathy, I say to him, "I read like an angel," JD, he'd cut me short, and still this drop of blood on the floor : that time I bled from my mouth or was it my finger, since then the silhouette of the word in the bushes in the late evening, Francis Bacon's *Jet of Water*, 1979, oil on canvas, on the tabletop 1 cup of tea steaming &c., Sacred Heart, I say, "*Le petit Jesus*," a few weeks after his death, I ran into Gert Jonke in Josefstädter Street and I could read on his face that he dreaded speaking to me and so we just walked past each other .... indeed I've always wanted to DEVOUR a whole book in a single day, didn't dare move since he was sitting next to me, I say, that time, the jasmine's white buds, still this drop of blood on the floor, I say namely in all the pink buds how can it be how can it have happened that the sm. weeds in the Schlossgasse (curbstone) the tiny daisies I mean the wall drawings of a pissoir : again and again past this pissoir after I passed this wilderness which brought me to tears, etc., <u>and finagled. Brilliant people</u> how the bell rang down at the gate late guests uninvited guests, I say, and at night trivial talents, "she said she was going to hang herself on the cherry tree in the garden if her eyes," said Renate K., the thought of 1 <u>bewildered bird-picture</u> : little bird bill ceremonious when will I become 1 swallow, find flowers and blindworms in the thicket and thistle-hair, sites of the flowering plant, IF I WERE TO DIE ....

ach this shadow in this garden : cypress-shadow, indeed still
shadow, little violet bird that's how they deal with me inscrutable
heavenly, flitting fauna TO THE SEA'S

28.3.12

I need to take care of SOMEONE this flowering plant on the cement floor this little jasmine plant in the kitchen, I say, tap its dirt with my finger to see if it's thirsty, or satisfied, it hugs and kisses me and we look at each other a long time, I'm responsible for this little jasmine plant, we whisper to each other .... "and the grass withers with all its beauty, but your word stands for ever .... wearing the tissue of our flesh he turned his eyes to us. He spoke words of love and inflamed our hearts, and now we hasten after the fragrance of his perfumes ...." Saint Augustine, *The Confessions* XIII, XV, then the loveliest arrowing of a rook over the rooftops of the city while the tender flesh of the cloud (spun out over the heavens) namely Renoir's pastel of a naked young woman with white gloves .... while a vagabond's secret sign on her door .... &c., while 1 drop of blood on the floor I'm bleeding from my mouth or finger, "for every calendar date 1 drop of blood, 1 drop of blood like the one you saw trickle over the back of the girl impassively letting herself be BUMfucked, turned to the radio, she knows ....," Jacques Derrida. Namely one of my ancestors, that <u>middle-aunt</u> who occasionally ruins my face, that is, my face in the mirror, when I see it I'm shocked and refuse to believe it, turn away from my ruined face in revulsion &c., and she, years later, <u>slides</u> out of her silk dress embroidered with poppies, <u>slides</u> lifeless to the floor <u>excreting</u> a drop of blood, &c.

And Father said, was it really necessary that I FLY, to Portugal or wherever, and I had no idea he would die in my absence, in my unscrupulousness, and so I insisted on going, wasn't it so .... since we, with Fellini, over the freshly swept grounds of the Naschmarkt I mean while 1 drop of blood on the pavement, from mouth and nose circa, the middle finger of the left hand, also cuckoo calls from the treetops of the little Danube woods, everything has gotten so overgrown, am shoreless, am here only temporarily, leaning on the window clasping myself to him, that beloved pale as silver, who in the star-clear heavens, who is wrapped up in mummy-bandages in a <u>fiery time of blossoming</u> (fleur)

29.3.12

Tàpies dead. Had me fooled, or whispering from the little garden ....

of a forest, circa, resumption of the dreams = tears from last night : rather damp meadows for Easter : while standing we entwined ourselves around each other like spring's branches from convoluted trees, I say, drunk ach, on Rose, delicately built language arts, say I, Thomas E., who turned away that day, do you remember, I say, we were sitting on the balcony at Roberta's .... (chick-restaurant)—I mean you bedded me down on the balcony under canopies : apparitions of the tenderest little forest, blooming linden branches entwined, raining willows, AND BIRD DUNG. Spellbound evening sky sinking stars I mean I saw how the moon <u>wandered</u> from west to east my fists wanted to hold him it didn't work, my tears. With Fellini on the grounds of the Naschmarkt .... ach in Weimar <u>dainty</u> (Swiss pine) : the sm. bed Goethe died in, &c., in the morning sticky eyelashes, I say, sticky morning moon = daymoon = crescent moon WAXING, I say, listening to your mournful voice in the morning, secret of loneliness (EvS), mild landscape of the heavens, ach black wool-tatters : outline of America on staff paper &c.

(we were standing with our bicycles at the Atlantic when the call came from home : they were standing with their bicycles before the waves of the Atlantic as the call from home .... am gone wild and overgrown everything in shoreless FLEUR,
<u>phlox and fetish, for Edith S.</u>)

31.3.12

Kuszmaul oboe, the darling dogs spent a long
time <u>chasing after</u> the wagon that was rolling
away, then fell behind : then gave up, then just
gazed after it : the dogs the horses (<u>lemurs</u>)

I ordered a <u>generalissimus</u> at the cafe = a sm. brown, utterly with-
ered flowers on the nightstand, and as if I were sitting before a
mirror I see my crude smile while one of the nice intellectual girls
asks me what I am reading, later, apparently the dream is set in
Berlin, I ask 1 other girl, possibly a <u>hermaphrodite</u>, how far it is
to the Grunewald so I might .... undisturbed, otherwise one
would have to do it right there on the street like a dog .... in the
cafe (see above) I had begun to write a text that enthralled me.
<u>Most of the dream</u> racing TATTERED like flying clouds that
altered within seconds &c., I sat with folded sensorium in the pas-
senger seat of our car and was staggered by the dark ragged locks
on the horizon that changed shape within seconds, and then we
were flying through 1 Ruisdael landscape .... do you remember
who I was, I say, I wrote <u>dance-poems</u> for you, that is, the society
of the dead : we look at them but they don't look at us, they just
make their exits and don't ever come back, ach so elliptical : verses
of the bushes in the hinterlands, &c., the be-thrushed spring, and
dripped hot tea on my knee, such 1 feeling of happiness that I'm
lying in your arms .... this my unbridled passion in the woods
of Berlin as we with Michael Hamburger (whose name I kept pro-
nouncing the German way), circa with wavering shadows and
draped with moss sinking into the softened forest floor, <u>aussi</u>, and
learned much from listening to the various heavenly beauties of
the fieldfare thrush, <u>for example, daffodil</u>—in a film we SAW

THE WIND : flying plastic bags, scraps of newspaper and little baskets : how else would one be able to see the wind, where it *did*

2.4.12

this tight textile, something comes to me, to my eye-
lids in the morning the dreams cling heavy are the
eyelids to which the dreams cling in the morning,
après-midi and fleur, nuage, I mean rose-twigs of
loneliness ach this ether (so that the elder should
be the servant of the younger .... Augustine, *The
Confessions* VII, IX)

these *lyrics* for the duration of the orgasm the soul leaves the body,
if I fold my hands the sacred knee, *ach bleib bei mir Herr Jesu Christ*
: miracle of the holy thorn whereas the finches <u>mostlovely</u>, you
know, in bushes with riven veins, hold me in the white blackthorn
my darling ach my Agnus Dei, and rushing in the bushes delirium
of love 1 buttercup dream 1 dale, and my language in a GRASS-
BUSH namely *les étoiles* and mallow-kisses most LOVELY ....
it's all collage = or bricolage, all reckoning, I mean we missed out,
summers, flying flowing fanning up the ramp of the <u>Albertina</u>, it
is the rod of my heavens : my heaven's cricket at the window
nights, chirping nightly at night in the atrium so that I can't find
sleep although I look for it for a long time, &c., also violets and
this shoot from .... purple-spring .... all over the city posters
with a photo of the world-famous Lotte Lehmann, glory of the
oriole and archangel pigeon, per Renate K., the leaflets of the aspen
the gossamer of the nights, the nights <u>executed</u>. The construction
rubble of my recollections, *sincerely* <u>my branchlets,</u> at 5 the birds'
vocalizations through the closed window, I lay awake the entire
night, I say, the teeming and the billing and cooing pulsed in my
chest &c. The locks I pushed in front of my eyes protected me from
the bright light when, interrupting my reading, I wanted to nap 1
little, stammering on the telephone the voice of Wolfgang E., the
1st violet bushes : colors and scents that moved me I mean through

one of the west-facing windows 1 smashing sunset (sweated blood circa), beyond the fence. The maple blossoms .... so I hung on his lips <u>while he always ran riot into my little heart</u> resting in the lap of God 1 <u>lark song</u> (= Johannes Brahms) : W.o.O. crying over it in German cursive 1 note—not decipherable—or I could sit a long time in the car crying with Ely like that, while on Ely's cheek .... namely in his staunch heart so that I copied what he had just said, I wrote and wrote as though I hoped to give up the ghost

6.4.12

in the tennis club. With battered bag to the <u>gym</u>. Managed to catch 1 stumbling girl. To recognize the essence of things, the body of language, howling isolation. <u>1 sound thrashing</u>, dealings with Brentano, tears passing away, the enchantment of heeding ....

I mean Helmut P. during a PEREGRINATION in the mountains/like Eichendorff's good-for-nothing <u>panting</u> 1 little = the peregrination of Helmut P., I say, peregrination in the mountains, panting 1 little, swinging his hiking stick, calling "Happy Easter" so that my throat I mean I choked, the boyfriend cozying up to others &c., how he, over the mountain, and panting 1 little as he called out "Happy Easter" to me so my throat constricted, oh my wailing as I listened to him as he with wavering voice and through the mountains (excretions/secretions in the pocket of the dressing gown) namely called out "Happy Easter" to me, which I in the rapture of nature = blaring of the birds he said I mean in the bullfinch copse he said "Happy Easter" on Maundy Thursday, I mean like blossoms that swim on the water, ach it made my throat close, he'd also read Joseph Roth to me, etc. But now it was as though he had embarked upon a long expedition, when actually he was just a few hours away what happened. It seemed to me, I say, as if he had gone far off although he was only a few hours distant (though he had distanced himself only by a few hours, what happened) .... I was bored or I didn't know what to do with myself, tuberose of Tuscany, from the GRAMO, I say. Sun and moon accompanied me, circa night-songs, <u>the clan</u> &c.

<u>Have on doll's dress</u>—living since the beginning of the year in <u>blossom-dust</u> = primrose path, I say, picked BERRIES from a hedge wild plants on paths so that melancholy nature only half

moved me. I am now in the habit, that. And fell on his neck, am a
pupil of repetition, harmless prattler (obscurantist), the scent of
blooming violet bouquets in the window and write and write as
though I hoped to give up my ghost (in his staunch heart, wasn't
it so)

8.4.12

she snapped while I stood, one arm <u>cushioned</u> against the wall,
and was a dancer. You are a dancer, she said, you are poetry. Photography
is 1 crash-angel : 1 poem : everyone should have a share
in this poem it should move everyone to tears. Poetry is 1
bloody branch, presented to ev'ry one

11.4.12

o lamb of the heart, nocturne and home-schooled like
so through the dusk .... emptied the cup of sleep : I
was thirsty .... "and where does it come from, the
flesh of the poem," asks Bodo H.

and am in free fall : am swallow am siskin am thrush. 1 nature walk
1 walking 1 peregrination as in the Vienna Woods, back then, with
giant steps, I say, we hadn't seen each other in a long time, I say,
namely poem that opens everything up. Singer sewing machine
over which, I mean, Mother bent sewing together scraps &c. Ach
these signs of erstwhile intimacy I was allowed to ride on his
lap, Haydn's stolen skull—because we could no longer frequent
each other <u>illness and death</u>, we talked on the telephone ½ the day,
circa harp music, should we get loafers for you, I say .... I think
I saw in the distance the 1st lilac bush, lilac-hued bushes then we
cried out, 1 freak : cataract of tears, I say, in the pergola, in the
caecilian bushes (Okopenko.), fleurs, étoiles, and nuages feelings
of inadequacy, long walk with Edith S. (14.4.12) in the grip of
winter, wound down the Wiedner Hauptstrasse, &c., I had on my
trench coat which the storm billowed, perforated night, Easter
checked off, Concor 5 and Lasix under my tongue, we were some-
thing of a duet, forget-me-nots springing up in the little fire garden
such that tears, fine mechanics still okay, old chestnut tree in the
Burggarten unfurled light-green leaves, you could believe we'd
spent our entire lives in the car, wrote JD, these CAHIERS are
1 book without progression, decades later, blue Danube, I send
you off in the car once more &c. very early I mean flanks of the
morning am so eager for each new day, so they ought to implore
me, I say, the cloud-flags in the wind, <u>like 1 glacis</u> in the morning
.... pan flute of fate : because one tends to judge the panicky lines

of the text as genius, it is wondrous how Plato's eye rolls forth and bulges and smokes, someone mentioned the name of an artist and I saw her picture before me (Colmar, from Chemnitz?), who called out to me, <u>in the inflammation of nature</u>, this ruffling that fit, that AFFRONTED me, wasn't it so ....

14.4.12

the mignonettes in the Augarten (back then), the two children, Rea and Manuel : jump rope and ball &c. or we sat on wooden benches at wooden tables while the treetops sweet breezes and flower garlands, now ever oftener from me fall …….. I mean objects from my hands, the little blond braids of the waitress at the Café Sperl who summers in the garden leaned a bit on a tree, so bushed &c., and I thought "she must be tired" or nerves of the woodlets …….. because before dawn the chirping of thousands = Jorie Graham, or 1 rain, senseless &c. I say, lilies, or, I'll walk behind you, which we laughed about as though the narrow <u>waves</u> of the public pool as you went under while the <u>waves</u> which twined around your face <u>undulated</u>, or in the sense of footsteps as I walked behind you, ever more slowly : scene of a spilling of tears, blossoms of the morning, little leaves of spring rustling, as we laughed : stumbled over the large roots, also sitting/sitting also in the meadows and deep valleys = Cobenzl …….. <u>ach sliding away</u> : <u>sliding into the day</u> so that I carried the finches into INDOLENCE, I mean as though I were daydreaming or as Jorie Graham says : MARRYING INTO (tears upon tears), as back then "little Elisabeth" MARRIED INTO in the Café Prückel, right? and she asked me if I had <u>1 intuition</u> for JD on the radio &c. and so I see through the occurrences of this world while Aslan Gültekin <u>fabulated</u> his gray hair back into a little braid. As with a girl to the dance &c., ach in the longing to live on, or like how we would pluck the petals of daisies and sing he loves me he loves me not, and would suffer when he did not love us. Oh we sat in the Drechsler, next to us they were laughing giggling, scarves *abandoned* = rejected cake with whipped cream (sparrows, arrows of yearning)—guillotine Amore, <u>slow in the windows</u>, torn like the nights, while the narrow moon pours itself out like those days in D. when I went around the garden at dusk with the tin watering can, ach in my fist the Cretan stone with the drawing BARRED BED, after Francis Bacon's *Studies of the Human Body* (1979)

15.4.12

1 spring's shower .... there was an Eng. author ("Springer")
he kept mentioning I mean each spring at the end of Laurenz-
gasse there was 1 tousled pair of lilac bushes, lilac and white,
whose organs were so high up one was hardly aware of their
fragrance .... we were sitting with a few women poets and one
of them was sketching the sumptuous tree of nature in the air
with her arms ("ach the bath cartridges") and comparing its
stature to the poetry we were writing .... while she was writing
the tree of poetry in the air, I really did see a tree, but it was 1
Mediterranean plant, probably a palm ....

Fontana, I thought, as I looked up at the sky which like old torn
silk I met Les Murray in the deep valleys, spring's shower. In the
drugstore e.g. I ran into 1 veiled young woman who looked familiar,
didn't know who she was or where I knew her from, then later, the
answer : it was the waitress at the Golden Lamb (on my street), ach
springing, Mahler's "2 blue eyes," we raced up the gloriette, here
Father's MERCEDES rolled down the high street, lost 1 wheel
&c. (21.4.12), I think I saw the 1st lilac in the distance, I say, oh the
nameless affliction. The other day listened to 1 radio play by Roland
Barthes, Lenchen had such a SWINGER on, had the gladiolas in
her breast pocket, spring's shower, they handle me like a child.
("étoile" and "fleur," thrush in apple tree .... goes very close to
the fence of the pub garden, plucks the weeds behind the fence
calls to the man busy behind it something like "circa, and are you
open this evening?" '27, Rubenspark, Grandmother's lotus hand
lifted me onto the park bench I was 3, namely grew dear .... ah
little heart ran riot with fear circa, deep-black blueberries how they
were the forest's "uncontrolled growth," or snacking on the wood-
beauties : infiltration of a love)

21.4.12

little soup of apricots = metamorphic thoughts, I
mean in the lap of tears .... "could
you please speak proper German,
I say to the Swiss poets declaiming
their poems on a hike through the Wachau,
so I can understand you" ....
ach to sew air on, I dreamed : memo,
NIGHTS with green pen &c.

brazzo : paw, of the painter Lorenzo Lotto (*Man with Golden Paw* from 1524?) and suchlike, we're sitting in the Drechsler where one feels the marvels of the day you know on my beloved's lap wasn't it so, we looked over to the little woods of the Naschmarkt where the Mediterranean fans unfolded <u>radiant</u> while we headfirst in a whirl .... ordered Goethe's *Italian Journey* (one goes under, one's ears stand on end = <u>I've taken leave of my senses</u>) ach out of the GRAMO sounds Satie, stenography <u>in the cahier</u>, languishing in the lace-up shoe, on the bedspread circa, familiar green copse, dead little dog headfirst <u>flower inflammation</u>, tracing the lady painter's blazer, &c. or "eye and hand fevering for unself" .... (anyway I kept stopping during our walk and attempting to <u>explicate</u> something with the help of my hands—I mean what I longed for—or as if I had an empty desk before me on which I was trying <u>I mean in vain</u> to put everything in its place, so we looked = we locked in, attempting to explain everything. Bent over I shuffle through the picture : that I crawled out of the car folding my hands sewing air on : summers in D., infinitesimal vocabulary, I say, which aggrieved me.) We sat in the little UPPER garden in Rome while the Rom. matrons walked by in their black garments little black bags tucked under their arms &c., and in the middle, Lenchen : my

little sword's unfathomable flower-sea's where feverishly strewn
butterflies ach sunken, ach sank into daydreams &c. spring's swans,
thrush in apple tree, I wake up : gripping pensée, I thought
Debussy, no, said Susanne B., insatiable little garden (millefleurs),
with so many flowers and ornaments, breathed in steep heavens,
snacking on springtide's harmonious shadows of night-beauties

24.4.12

"the eyne of flowers" .... I saw how the moon behind a gauze of tears &c., it rained in the night and I lay there alone. The invisible Loire, ach. I stood on the balcony "le kitsch," and from the glittering tip of the mountain opposite, the boyfriend called my name and waved. In February when the trees were still bare we asked ourselves whether we would ever see them green again .... full of fields and flames of high summer the dreaming-away of time, we're sitting in the Drechsler looking over at the Naschmarkt's little woods where the Mediterranean fans you know swishing in the wind unfold I read in G.'s *Italian Journey*. The white tennis shoes white candles in the window, agitated dreams, we prance through the emptied Naschmarkt, the curtains you know totally somnambulistic, withered in the CAHIER delicate birds and <u>violet-wise</u> "drifting off and hanging on his lips," JD, and violet-wise hung on your lips, hey! Moor-tongue! tonguelet, howling, we will greet each other, back and forth, we crept up the Cobenzl footpath, sat in the little upper garden, amid .... teeming butterflies tumbling into the mignonettes, in the pergola in the periphery the budding, branchlets, in a glass the dying lilies of the valley, the flanks, birdlet on the green silhouette of the mountains, from the window &c. Came from the mountains that day and violet-wise he grabbed my breast, I say, 1 freak = cataract of tears, I say, I was still little. Like 1 glacis, in the morning

7.5.12

the sm. girls in the photographs keep walking past the feet of the bride and groom while the kiss of the white-naped honeyeater, in the mountains, while the cabbage whites chased us down, in the morning I had dipped my hair into 1 jar of honey &c., we looked at ourselves in the mirror and I saw that my beloved had brown eyes but mine were bright blue, I mean we both had <u>deep rose-eclipses</u> in our eyes .... ach now the fire's burning = he is 1 fanatic, Michael L. .... toward morning I had a dream I was sleeping with him in a wooden hut with 1 sm. window facing a garden of irises it was spring and the spring wind gusted around us but when we kissed I awoke, with an ache in my chest. My beloved was Jean Genet but I thought it was 1 French film star from the '30s, actually I had dreamed of P.W. I couldn't remember what I had whispered into his ear, in the corner (in the crook) of the wooden hut 1 elderberry tree, circa, 1 PARAPLUIE, that *was* the green one in the rose garden, I say, 1 lilac done blooming, you know, I tear my eyes out of my head I cry my eyes out, &c., 1 blue foxglove bush, the moon's apparent pendulum. The heavens held us : fatuous earth, soul-bird .... in May the thrush so spring festival years ago namely as spring set in as the chestnut trees bloomed. The rare is the desirable because the dead man his guise because the chestnut tree its red blossoms because <u>the green bushes</u> edging the street .... the Spaniards photographed the rain because it was 1 welcome occurrence because it had not rained in such a long time, oh erratic person what are you of a dark-blood mignonettes, ach the invisible Loire, from the window, birdlets on the mountains' silhouette, and violet-wise I hung on his lips, benevolent nights budding branchlet you seek the truth of language (1 freak 1 cataract of tears) .... <u>I feel beholden to Mannerism</u>

16.5.12

plate of cherries untouched, I see the <u>NULLEST star</u>, &c.

there used to be these days of warm rain and on clear nights the stars' initials, these little tails of .... book-spiders in my bed, longing for faraway friends, the taste of regret and shame &c., I'm an *underdog*, Beuys's "Stone Rabbit" it moved me &c., that time in D. the leap into the village canal where glass shards cut my foot, insignificant autobiographies of other people, litanies of tears, Hochstrahl fountain in white, so I carried the finches into the day and <u>protégée</u>, long walk in Votivpark with MAMA (18.5.12), write only the impossible, JD, <u>his foot which was 1 bit crooked with noble firs</u> .... ach Haydn's, springing up in the little fire garden (fetch CD from the city // spider in bed) where miracle of memory in the lap of tears, climbing the stairs each night my eye roves involuntarily over to the courtyard window where day and night 1 light is burning, presumably someone terminally ill in bed while from behind a door some horn concert of Joseph Haydn I mean Haydn's : rather excruciating just now .... transverse flute, harpsichord .... dream of Duchamp's chess game .... ach flowers impuissance Lorenzo Lotto's paw or how she, Angelika K., clattered over hill and dale in her car .... wishing I were home with eyes closed the meager repast then at the little folding table wolfing it down and at the same time falling into a deep sleep Bach's sons and "*trophy*" : hornbeams in allées, burst of tears, I sit there on a sweet May day, 1 bit enclosed while hues of blue and fortissimo of feelings, I imagine last year's bird's nest in the night bushes at the Naschmarkt (empty &c.), he said "not too soon," which meant don't come back too soon .... o I ought not go into decline : underpinning my instinct = spirit-body through soul-bird, oh I

should never go into decline, soul-bird's insinuation, right—fleur
and bed of grass back then under bushes, on the day the 1st person
flew to the moon I visited him in the hospital garden, and he, as
farewell in his little notebook (underlined: encrypted)

19.5.12

all your sm. shoulders fleur and cahier in my asylum
or CROCO I mean Haydn's, hornbeams in the allées
I mean "trophy" by Leon Golub I mean nature's
ataxia before my eyes, leaning out the open window,
the window frame's wood dabbing tears dabbing
.... 1 footpath, sm. forest path lined with spruce
needles like a slippery mat I walk down in this green
cathedral, in this cathedral (in whose poem) the forest
birdlets, twittering fragrant landed on my ring finger
&c. as though they were my soul-friends, so I hurried
(darted) down the fading carpet of flowers in this
green cathedral and the dusk light fell at my feet while
rosy shadows of the roses deer and caterpillars, kissed
the deer's seed which was <u>so ornamental</u> .... said
CORA, this the name of the poet's wife, you know,
who had <u>torticollis</u> (decline) .... with frugal curl the
little bird, little wellspring and deep grotto (fleur and
étoile) while the air-comrades in the aisles while the
black cat held 1 Jew's harp to its <u>mouth</u> with its left
paw (in weird terrycloth &c.)

<u>and there are also always those down days when one nearly
despairs</u> :

whereas the flambéed boy whereas moonbeams tumbling into the
allée &c. it made me blanch ach tiny gulch the Virgin Mary
DRAWS NIGH

21.5.12

Bach on the gramo, song of the spider, I showed her how big the spider was, I mean it hopped down from the book pile oh in this improbable way, the next morning if it was 1 clear day we'd see the Pyrenees, etc., later, big impulse, the pale ringlets of the lion in my dream its megaheart, that night we set out into the apricot garden, gardenlet, crying, while the storm, my flatbreast, I do believe it will go on : <u>heart chirrups</u>, I want to dedicate .... the "études," all your sm. shoulders in my exile or CROCO, there are also always those DOWN days when one nearly despairs, my mother has been dead a long time but her love is so fond, I say, don't want to die on a May day like this, so I rushed into the green Danube where fading flower-carpets swam .... ach you'll be lost to me, I'll look for you everywhere and find you nowhere, I mean we'll never hold each other again entwined in the Augarten namely accompanying the sinking sun, actually wrapping while the 1st <u>flitting</u> star, that is, lost in the deep grotto, right, decayed in the <u>cahier, fumbling</u> "59" comma, em-dash, flesh of the clouds I mean Renoir's pastels <u>I wake up and the morning shimmers</u>. He was 1 paterfamilias, and commanding, she said, landscape with cow, I say, a vision in spring, you're EVENING BEAUTY, says Michael Heltau .... <u>drunk, ach 1 rose</u>, crescent moon WAXING, am wildly overgrown, <u>as if I were flying</u> : drop of blood Portugal &c.

leaning on the window, enveloping the silver-pale which in a fiery flowering "fleur" (wrapped up in mummy-bandages) .... with folded hands, I say, <u>stormy forest tatterlet</u>

(dabbed my eye/until it hurt)

23.5.12

stormy forest tatterlet, wind-yoke &c., 1 "underwood" by Edgar Degas, rapture of the moon &c., back then he took me like 1 flower = daffodil, under his arms, lifted me high and bedded me on the divan .... during the dancing mania. You were lost that time and wandering between cheek and lip but then you kissed only my cheek, I was hoping for my mouth, anyway a few thorns I rushed into the green Danube where MOMENTARILY, &c., am wildly overgrown in my exile or CROCO where birdlets shimmered, presumably (jubilated), green silk leaves on my back, silk greenery .... silk sweater and his hand between the silk sweater and my back, I know your body the most, I know your body more lovingly than any other body .... I went to see him at the cemetery with a little stool you know : little folding stool I could cry my eyes out on you know (trimmed the rose-heads the daffodils), sat there on the folding stool at the edge of his grave, didn't I, this white shadow of the opened petals of the white lilies, with folded hands, I say, phlox and fetish and fleur we had twined around each other standing, you bedded me in the tender holt, etc., 1 Haydn I did not like on the GRAMO, millefleurs, insatiable little gardens that had me fooled .... headfirst and LANGUISHING flower-inflammation in the cahier

I mean that the tears SCURRIED that then the tears scurried .... *in the cloud* &c., that time and so many thorns, I rushed down the green Danube, so momentarily &c., ach summers in D. ran down the main street in Jesus sandals to the embellishments of the coltsfoot petals .... I was in a delirium was so delirious oh that the troubled, oh while the troubled garden of the soul pulsed through me ach me, schoolgirl's pleat, speechless am I tuft of grass little root, moon as stalker, and as we hiked along the sunshine it occurred to me that the man sitting next to me in the restaurant had had no left arm and I was startled my beloved made the selfsame observation, or when the moon seemed so close I could touch it and over its magical hair/head (high, in the folds of its robe), which is to say, CREDENZAS, ruby-red flecklet of sun on wardrobe &c., while the cherry-blood of your cheek namely since we were in the shadow of that petal : <u>clothed</u> in white, wasn't it

29.5.12

like characters in a play : he and she, striding slowly along, across the Hauptstrasse, hiding the car keys at his back I mean, the ringlets, their pick-up sticks, the inexorable path across the street he and she as in a dream as in perpetuity I mean they cross the street he and she without abiding they cross the Hauptstrasse striding slowly along, on the horizon, don't they, with Pentecost leaves the crowns of their heads, striding slowly without abiding, meanwhile the heavens, and evermore

30.5.12

empathy for a <u>half-sucked</u> cherry pit in the open kitchen drawer meanwhile the cloudlets : gray cloudlets dive down, tumble down and sea calm in the paintings of Claude Lorrain, presumably small lump of humanity, presumably from the gramophone Bach's Cantata 199 bird languages in the afternoon &c. .... always with one foot in clumsiness (filthiness) <u>there were antlers</u>, but in the shade 1 little calf, hillsides covered in liverwort ....

"Am Tabor," we'll find it with the GPS, etc.

it was 1 romantic relationship, no superfluous words, he was carrying an old backpack : don't go with your backpack into strange dwellings (Barbara F.), he played piano while standing, at concerts, his womanly profile (as in the film) with mouth ajar, his thoughts spoken in voiceover ("she hadn't told me the weather forecast for the coming days .... I need a vacation in the mountains, glaciers, skiing, etc. ..") 1 network, X-rated &c. He, giving a concert, standing at the grand piano, his womanly profile, mouth ajar, his thoughts spoken in voiceover as in a film, I mean no hope of gaining a foothold as a post-surrealist poet in the Fr. tradition, these days of a week don't give out, nestled into him I read a little in his MS which he had on his lap and couldn't help thinking of his PHOENIX .... bird's nest from last year in the tree crown reanimating I mean <u>maddest</u> (soughing), I mean down in the <u>depths of the park</u> as we strolled past it &c.

circa dirty jokes (wounds)

(1 very still bright day in the window, the forget-me-nots of your eyes, "no one saw through the purple," JD)

5.6.12

composed at 4 o'clock in the morning because the green gar-
lands of John Dowland : countertenor's ringlets with murky
eye, gauze of tears, to sink with one foot into misfortune, back
then 1 outbreak of feelings you went with bloody branchlets at
your feet it was summer and it was in B., language dictates what
we have to say, not OTHERWISE ....

always in the crook of the arm. Bit of dampness in the morning,
rosebud red .... that time with Siglinde B. took the footpath from
the hospital (where Mother was) to the nearby station, and I asked
if she wanted to take care of Mother later, when she was back
home, to which she replied, yes .... well anyway.

Ach the big ravens' bills switched out, right .... meditation in the
woods, the doctor said, copper beeches, crescent moon, night sky
starless for weeks, 4 o'clock in the morning the first writing, right
eye darkened, everything stained mauve, wealth of ideas stream of
tears, recollections of love (in the bar of the Hotel Sacher with
friends : illusory worlds, unfamiliar, cold June, Kieser training,
Venus a dot before the sun today, immense pent-up feelings ....
plucketh out the eye, the eye doctor says, the tapered eye, the
poems of Ernst Meister, the little laurel tree on the terrace, I mean
the torment of making a decision)

the serrated writing of the Cretan sea, per Edith S.

6.6.12

ambivalent, the encounter with Belgian poet William Cliff =
pseudonym for André Imberechts .... after his reading his stiff
face came to life. He walked up to me and I said to him, I'm a
post-Surrealist : he did not approve, and shook his head.
Between the pages of his poetry book *L'État belge*, 1 pressed
gingko leaf &c.

a bit damp ach! in the quarters. Long-lived lucky as if emerging
from the hereafter spouse niece butterfly, on the Hauptstrasse,
moon, jagged nights (*working*, with a sharp vegetable knife)
<u>accompanied</u> in the afternoon past the bouquets .... didn't
recognize her, thin-lipped, on a visit to Vienna, memory deep
as a well : Georg, Bibi, Maria. Eye veiled, Corpus Christi, in the
shop window peony, rosebush, soil, <u>that's where we always
parked</u> &c.

(1 rosé-colored ribbon on the parquet floor)

7.6.12

I was doing okay the whole time but now, the stars in the train win-
dow <u>twitter</u>, he looks into the car window and asks something, I
mean 1 kaleidoscope this world, in stormy rain lightning and
thunder, always as though I understood what you had said but I
understand nothing, am in a dark wood beloved, no one can help
me not even you, in thunder and lightning Peter W. always looks
into the car, of course, underneath his umbrella &c. I did something
wrong, you know, I <u>exaggerated</u> something or other, tears like cor-
uscating stars = Puccini, there's no hope for it, whenever it is windy
and raining Peter W., hunched over, looks into the car ....

we find flowers, <u>solemnly</u>, pre-consummated in the dream : oper-
ation on my right eye transit of Venus before the sun, ach I awaken
from the rushing of the rain, protegée, I see you through cloud
forests, elliptical sentences, snug snow .... I live in symbiosis
with violet blossoms and amid the thorns (which wolfed me down)
.... <u>to the consecration</u>, I mean I order something to eat to drink
but I don't want to either eat or drink (everything was tolerable
up to now) .... he kissed me and 1 dewdrop fell from his fore-
head into my heart, &c., 1 pergola of wisteria, per JD, a bit damp,
fleur or GLAS (death knell), am unreadable have become invisi-
ble, little bell of the clitoris, Jean Genet, he says, something like
free-floating fears, and in a little basket the ripped-up (half) book,
there are flower bouquets in your eye, there are flower bouquets
of my fear in flames, &c., when we drive by your house we always
wave up to your window, the one with the curtains, but sometimes
you are standing at the gate, and wave back. Namely just so that,
day after day and year after year, <u>omens are blooming</u> in this
boundless blossomtime

11.6.12

there in the corner the bush, is green embushed this morning is
green this morning ach little green pigeon early morning through
the crack of the embushed window it's a June morning IMAGE is
FLEUR and CAHIER, it's quiet this morning embushed dreams
(ambivalent) bosquet .... 1x he told me she had kneeled at his
door : imploring him to love her (*so on* . . .) ach the morning light
so <u>poignant</u> curtains and little grass fleur and nuage, jasmine on
the stairs, you know, my lamb, effervescing water in my chest &c.,
"<u>let's cruise!</u>" he says, "on the horizon!," John Dowland's breaths,
snippets of Stefanie snippets of midriff, you know, I was delirious
&c. these waves, you know, these dragonflies, my foot wilts me :
my heart, speechless am I, grass-bushel little root, moon as stalker
<u>I know in the bottommost drawer of the armoire my memory</u>
<u>in the mailbox the bird's nest &c.</u>

<u>insignias, of the dog on the tiled floor before he exhaled his soul</u>
= FLOCKI

(today I won't go for a long <u>walk</u> I'd rather be <u>at the window,</u>
<u>leaning, and wilt into</u> the bushy swing ride of the hills on the
horizon, &c.)

15.6.12

Lily's purse, for Samuel Rachl

in the Prado in the Rüdigerhof, the moon's tenderest jetty in the
night sky (the lake), while in the ivory-colored air <u>Lily's purse</u> :
little spring, fledgling dove, traces of a feeling &c. allegro of the
early morning and I find a flower, festive, fleur, to the consecra-
tion, you have little fire-hands : Lily, the designer, on the sidewalk
at New Year's with her little purse .... little chamomile flower
dunked in water, and I, drifting through the morning as once in
D., when I was 1 child with gorse blossoms .... here he = Hans
H. said "My fledgling dove" while crossing the Stubenring,
namely he said, "My fledgling dove gets worried when it flutters
. . . " ach Lily with her purse, fledgling dove, how Hans H. whis-
pered to me, "My fledgling dove always says," said Hans H., "it's
worried about me." Lily namely with her purse she designed
herself, CIRCA potato print, CIRCA doll's kitchen, are those lily
stems or green pens?

but now it was as though melancholic nature had taken me to her
breast for the consecration namely, fleur or nuage, now it was as
though my tears would never dry, while Lily, the fledgling dove,
on the Stubenring accompanied by her purse .... the woodlets
by the Danube namely, with her black PLASTIC purse, right, <u>ach
I have a car full of drums</u>, was at Beckmann's and sport-flowers,
fairylike, out of my body's orchard (JD), am very symbiotic

(<u>I still have 1 lantern, or, the love affair</u>)

19.6.12

dear Prof. Beck, it was in winter, on the stairs to Prof. Heilig's office, that we (ran) into each other—didn't recognize you at first—and now it is high summer, the time when I always go in for a checkup. This year I want to postpone my visit to the fall .... at the Confra. There *was* something about cherries, I didn't note it down, the 1st half of the year <u>flew by, ach featherlet in the wind</u> &c., we had taken a long walk, it popped up and I hoped I'd be able to remember it but the next morning it was gone : inkling of cherries, gentle rain (with barrette and bangs styled to the side as documented on 1 photo from childhood, &c.)

She was a milliner, and had dark wooden model heads .... pines and cypresses, made a present of one to a friend along with the old GRAMO, in the field full of thistle 1 rapture, Picasso's little bull, flung myself around his neck in the bullfinch copse, didn't I .... I mean doing cartwheels on the Rialto Bridge or this thought that imposed itself during a walk in the sun, that one could hear the grass grow : goldfinch, lily factor, I see eyes all over .... today I won't go for much of a walk, would rather lean on the window, <u>that is, enter into bushy half-sleep, &c.</u>, with <u>jagged hair</u>, the philosopher, who ....

(oh that the insatiable garden flooded through me)

25.6.12

obstinate ONLINE, cautious prosthesis : eye prosthesis shaggy like night, ivy and peony bud for the festivities, ach to sew on air like song, lily of the valley rolling like tears May and June, flown away the blood-red garments of July, but now it was as though the rustling meadow had taken me in its arms, lily of the valley and branchlet, fleur and nuages, with stiff strands of hair in a black garment the figure of the painter and philosopher (90 carrier pigeons perished in a fire), I have become mouthless : language-less, as <u>back then</u> in Rome I, the wisteria woods <u>back then</u> the bare star &c. of Agamben the friend spoke I nodded in agreement, as if I knew what he was talking about, trellis of pink vetch, gerbera daisies (with wrapped stem, like Frida Kahlo) .... your voice so throstle, fir mountains to and fro, you sat at the desk and talked on the phone, with jagged hair the philosopher or painter = Samuel Rachl, with *sneakers* and patientia .... my god : will kick the bucket : it's far from over, wool blankets for miles, banal questions of .... I want to walk in the woods &c., while melancholy (lawn), <u>wrench open the eye, the bestial one</u>, I was almost asphyxiated (breastlet) ....

"Come, here are the flowers, and see on the left these beds of sweet grapes, soul's coloratura," that time we swirled out of the house and up the hillside the little fire-hand with SEMEN'S .... (pluck out my eye so it can't cry anymore, Flanders poppy and painting), pastose nature, strands of hair, <u>biting, the dust</u> .... snug snow, &c.

<u>ach ach the likes of you</u>   (desert of irascibility)

           (I'm inhaling Tipp-ex)

27.6.12

ach the shadow-play of dreams, the night amid it, how erect the firs. When she got lost, she would call to her grandfather = forester for help, could he please <u>release</u> her from the woods .... scent of sweet woodruff, blossoming primroses and violets, sat down and listened to the river ("slaughtered"), the pleated, impassioned waters. As Hollywood = fairy tale, procession of ants, wasp on the tongue : like Marcel Beyer wrote in his poem .... sunrise–sunset at the edge of the woods, 4-leaf clover and mushrooms, birdlet in the crowns of the trees her song, nightingale, cried (I), little blond braid Tyrol, cherry cheeks and lips, and summers, rainy day : brunette idyll. How I longed for <u>affection</u>, I mean episodes of the tongue in his <u>bush</u> <u>= bouche</u> &c., plankton of the eye .... reflected in the kettle : a shrunken head, neurosis, ask the doctor, VIOLA VIOLA

<u>am too weary to slice open the eye-bags</u>
for Sabine Groschup's little Tyrolean braid

28.6.12

<u>Note on *HEIM* : video animation, 16 : 9, HD, stereo, 11 min. 40
seconds, by Claudia Larcher</u>

architecture, for example, glass harp, archive of the attic, machine
gun in the parents' bedroom. Delirium cellar, sights aimed out-
doors. Shrouded lawn mower, photos and breezes Claudia
Larcher's. I mean all sorts of birds in it, earth's shadows under
cedars in bloody boughs ....

iron-curtain garage door with a bang : end of the intuition

4.7.12

and snowflaked the woods &c., lambkin namely of a lesser home, learned e.g. from the swift-descending dusk that the summer WEEPING I mean WANING, the fall BOLSTERING, in these woods where finches namely in sparse crowns, where delicate shadows, where we <u>strolled</u> with cautious = large steps, ach little rivulet, blossom-sea Dufy, I mean sweet going-to-seed, I sleep till late in the morning, maybe it is also a child's longing, how I love the woods, the open air—like back then in D., when I was 1 child on the leas, melancholia, elderberry bush, while you .... and I say to Nurse H. "this little fountain on your body, saucers on both sides, &c.," ruffling of the season .... fresh like forget-me-not it bound me to you LILAC, and carrying the little violet bouquet in my other hand, JD in "Glas" .... when we were on that reading tour through France, we also went to <u>Parma</u>, and we met 1 university professor from Parma, actually, <u>it was all a dream</u>.

The panicle the chrysanthemum, on his birthday, once a year = 3.9., I gave him a bouquet of chrysanthemums : mauve miracle, my messiness with the electric lamp which means, for example, that objects fall from my hands like Passions .... and Simon introduced him to me, whispering, "This is Georg," tall handsome man &c., and I learned that Simon had introduced this Georg to you by whispering, "This is Georg," serious young man, tall, witty &c., "Mayröck" sounds like "lilac" he said, You are a dancer, which was vexing, head tilted to the left in the photo, edifyingly following my own pattern. That's when I learned that I was in such a <u>sphere</u> that I was not in a position to speak, finding myself in a chrysalis, I mean head tilted to the left, hearkening .... as the blueberries the heavy hedges I mean as I <u>stormed</u> up the slope so the thorns or underbrush on my skin &c., like this morning, the poisonous blue thunderbolts of the blissful cuckoo, always these <u>neologisms</u>, left eye blurred, I lapped up the little jasmine plant, sometimes the snow-mountain $= 1$ apparition and more, Bernadette H., while nut trees towered clouds before our eyes .... on a sm. drop of water, with flame-radiance

8.7.12

.

I have 2 hands
I have 2 arms
I have 2 feet
I have 2 legs
I have 2 ears
I have 2 lips
I have 1 eye

when I linger in the garden
I'm enraptured by writing
the mother's hands are riven
but the Virgin Mary DRAWS NIGH

when I was sick you
came to visit me when I
couldn't see you guided
me when I was afraid
you encouraged me
when I cried you consoled
me when I was
tired you carried me

1 breastlet summer puff 1 tatterlet of lion and roses strewn
in the allée while flambéed bird tender
moon ach little thunder-flower dimly <u>the eye-bags</u>
cut through, and violas

for Edith S.
14.7.12

white rainy-day kisses of dew, blossoms Dufy, while writing I'm enraptured, it's raining fire-flecks, my skin, my hand as if I had gloves on that were too big for me ach banderoles, ach it's raining fire-drops ach generic drugs, ach the July days flecking me, *mouches volantes*, you are acting like 1 child, you're thirsty, and you've just left the house, back then when I was 1 child I ran around in the garden in D. I mean little foehn .... susurrant then, MONET, did time transform into your soul, 1 bit susurrant and then metamorphosing from the general to the specific (hope my lantern will be true!) .... and like 1 thunderbolt the shadow of a bird whooshed over me, on my knees before the machine : 1 Glenn Gould, &c. But downright pleasant in a cafe, sun glittering through curtains .... steaming morning .... I flip out .... giant UNDERDOG with lady, ah fairylike : little eye-bags and violas sliced through, I wanted to devour the banderoles from your mouth, your thinking heart, soul coloratura. How we did it. How it beclouded. Today won't go for a long walk would rather lean longingly at the window or enter into bushy half-sleep, with white *SNEAKERS* with patina (how much time did we spend looking for that word), I mean moon-night : not knowing about me, my beloved's CURL, and flecked : someone would fleck me, wouldn't they, while I slept with Melos and wafted away Lord, if I now, if the other eye gets cloudy &c., we ran into each other, poppy and thimble, new colors after the operation, now it was as though tender Nature had flung her little arms around me .... innocent lip on which the snowflake melts

neige nuage, last sequence of a long dream : you sat down at your desk and talked on the phone, white tears, I haven't see you in a long time I haven't held you in a long time, where might you be

25.7.12

how reprehensible. But the gramo bellows. Today I'm staying inside myself, no fawning faltering .... he doesn't betray his thoughts, which leaves him lonely, &c., he led me through the John Cage exhibition and finally I sank down onto a wooden bench in the interior of the little summerhouse there where his tools were in a row .... was he 1 friend? .... Enough. I howl my eyes out, the one I love no longer loves me the high summer suffocates my heart, jargon of ardor. Flowers dreaming like snowflakes, gala of the queen anne's lace, vis-à-vis the moss on flat roofs, the new colors, the stammering, the anxiety, and at night thunderstorms : God's monumental finger jutting out of storm clouds as if painted by Goya .... to gorge and to howl 1 dozing .... that time he lifted me onto his bare feet = bear paws and carried me around the room, these affections repeated with the other woman &c., behind the "blinds" the seductions of the summer night, the tempestuous heart. Writing down again and again on a notepad : "To church!" .... Jacques Derrida's circumcision (I mean I'm governed by not-knowing, or that time on the Miami coast <u>the Atlantic rose up and the rosebushes</u>

26.7.12

the green bosquets I mean bushes I mean the little nipple your
theater cloak, I say, some sort of longing, say I, the departing
forest-bouquets of infatuated sycamores, lily of the valley sweet
woodruff springs abstract ecstasies, <u>am cuckoo</u>, in the midst of
the lilac bush, I spliced VIOLET, veiled branchlet

imperative vegetable I mean from the past I dreamed of the past
ach into the river that branched, 1 certain type of field-flower.
Fleurs. Stomach acidic, a word or phrase from somewhere or other
maybe from a dream, <u>flowerlet-sex</u>, my seeing-slits inflamed, we
were standing at night by the neighbor's garden where the blue
phlox I remember the blue waft &c., they were friends I mean full
moon almost full moon : silver lump of moon, was I suffering
romanesquely? this garden with the moving phlox I remember,
on the paths to the garden little apples with bites taken out of them
in the grass tiny and green, it was quarters of an hour it was 1
night, the little girl Marie, the bullfinch copse, we brushed through
the woods looking for mushrooms, the neighbor's garden we stood
there with our friends it was night it was a summer night with the
blue eyes of the phlox and on the paths the little apples I think with
bites taken out I wanted to bend over wanted to <u>gather</u> them, locks
of the stars, we stood there with our friends the phlox had opened
its blue eyes, no one spoke, maybe whispered I mean on that summer
night in Bad Ischl, the little garden with the phlox softly moving,
although I was tired I wrote everything down, etc., 1 silver lump
of moon and these words came, these phrases from somewhere
like the coltsfoot petals in D., back then with Mother in the inner
courtyard, and Father's motorcycle (quirt, carriage, and starry
sky) back then in D., I remember, lonely melodies and branchlet

Imagination, I mean Arnulf Rainer's riven face, staring at the ceiling .... so that I come back to life, the wave-line of his mouth, took readings fairylike of the temperature of things, while the nut trees towered up clouds before my eyes ach my blissful cuckoo, little blissful cuckoo my agave, <u>the VIPs namely</u>, in the yapping woods, proëm from the same day &c., I had chest-antlers, flew like 1 Oslo, it flooded through me insatiable stars .... am insensate 1 désir

31.7.12

ach pansy's breathlessness unkempt summer, vivid dreams, why at exactly that instant did 1 eyelash (fall) from your left eye, broken free from your eyelid, <u>lion in the neighborhood</u>, &c., the boys carried away my manuscripts by the suitcase &c., the beloved locked my door with his key, I slipped on an old black crepe-de-chine dress, was rejuvenated, she rejected me nevertheless, excellent mother–son relationship ....

Scissors on the nightstand meant : <u>I'm expecting letters</u>, I was pleased with my boldness to him as we loped off through shaggy bushes, free-floating anxieties. I mean Gerhard Richter's *Bouquet*, 2009, 60 x 88.5 cm, meditative flowers in yellow. His *Venice* : pointillistic black barque or swan as copy on tatty bedsheet, jeune = yellow banner, remote bushes, red elated sailboat, I mean best wishes and dead mosquito .... I have such a gleam yellow gleam in the corner of my eye, like a yellow eyelash .... ach in the swaddling bush how the valleys twinkled ....

(<u>this little tub</u> in which once 1 bouquet of yellow roses refreshed itself <u>most sumptuously</u> in the water : 1 gift from my publisher : but now it collects wastepaper, I mean curious transformation, while 1 most wistful silver lump of full moon appears in the window as Bach is playing <u>adornment</u> of the flower-denticles of Gerhard Richter. Jawlensky's *Girl with Sash*—ach gleam of elder-flower, "*mon cher catholique*," high summer's namely dwindling forest-bouquets ....

<u>1 halcyon day 1 half-carafe</u>

fairylike across the ear, at which I came back to life, temperaments of the fir-blue, yellow bunting, salamander, lily, <u>the notebook from Nice</u> rotted on the privy, &c., this summer in flames, clover and cuckoos namely, proëm from the same day, sometimes snow-mountains : 1 apparition and more, Bernadette H., I mean nuage, and cahier, I mean fleur and fire and <u>lantern</u> = my countenance, something familiar, she says, my harness,

1.8.12

I mean .... silken blue comet's tail of my thought, my room in the morning everything in blue, blue towels and petals, the wood floor of the room strewn with catkins you know, my life hung by a thread you know, I am very lonely but I have these secrets, I used to admire the photographs of your sister, Thackeray, I'm very narcissistic. That time in Budapest, half-waking half-sleeping with a bouquet of flowers in my hand .... dumbstruck am I : grass tufts little rootlet roundelay of the mountains, we walked into each other's arms .... ach and if she drown'd .... praise god 1 spleen of pink vetch landscape of pears fleur and nuage little birds on rivers, sweet woodruff fragrant primrose and violet, sat down and listened to the river, which .... (slaughtered) he was to release her from the woods, the dreams amid, but now it seemed to me as fairylike, as though my tears would never dry, little brunette shovelful of earth, maybe I could drink a rain, how velvety your eye, "And how kindly you speak," Adalbert Stifter, quoted by Anja Utler, "and how blue are your eyes," I heard his voice, and protégée, elderberry bushes all around, blessed beech grove immense in space, wasn't it, am writing a lot, my own poems, little eye-pillows squinting, I say, tiger lily on my chest &c., ach and if she drown'd, pink espalier, joyful as ascetics we whirled around, well, columbine and bracken bushes, pleated waters, snug snow, I folded my hands, a few weeks ago = in early summer you know as the rosebushes in the Volksgarten and in the middle the enormous linden tree spread out its arms and then I understood that we all must keep our secrets for ourselves, and crashed to the ground, with jagged hair 1 Tieck, oh I see it wandering like a ghost : tatterlets of summer breeze .... (didn't

want you to flatter me ....), circa doll's kitchen ach. <u>We split
the grub &c.</u>, and I waded through papers

6.8.12

<u>on</u> : Sebastian Isepp *Edge of Woods in Snow*, 1910–11, oil on canvas, 75 x 93 cm

leave it out, leave it out—gullet of the privet : bitter snow ....
ach I mean crunching in snow as I walked in snowshoes one step
at a time through the pink winter day &c., I mean I'm coming
from the left and as I brush the snow-covered branches the tree
shudders and <u>snorting puffing</u> casts off its sumptuous pelt, like
young soft antlers I think the velvet or down of young roebucks,
stags .... and advancing dumbstruck into the ice-blue interior
of the woods : my God like 1 lake of sentimental waters as if one
were standing at its rim (edgiest edge / tones from the pianino) and
I dove down into the icy depths didn't I. Fantasizing, fragile sheet
of ice : ice skating rink as once, as 1 child &c., pirouetting on the
Gusshausplatz while crows circled over the child's head, cawing,
then plummeted down to the child and pulled it up into the crys-
talline airs (see Arnulf Rainer's painting), oh how frantic, fright-
ened the child. Then back, crunching steps, arms swinging upward
into the veiled heavens where silver bells I mean white gladiolas
warn of the dangers of drowning, iris, mignonette, galactic
phlegm, veil of galaxies, ere the evening sank &c. I trudged back
through the snow, <u>and protégée</u> .... with a little branch I wrote
(for example) the word ROSE in the snow, and who have we here,
erring this way?, Virgin of Mercy new snow oh what ghosted
through me—there! 1 phantom : 1 white bell : 1 little bell bending
to the ground : 1 snowdrop, as though it were already an envoy of
early spring .... ach crashed to the ground, rose, mignonette,
daydreamed sweet woodruff primrose and violet, do you remem-
ber, that time in Perchtoldsdorf when we saw the foxgloves or

foxes, I mean the peonies bought on the sly, in the meadows while BE-GLOVED hand I mean &c. through the mesh of the park fence. Anyway I slept into the morning and in my dream I said to myself, you're a fatalist, then found 1 <u>wild</u> leaf from last fall in the snow : brown gingko leaf in a hollow, and sinking down in an ecstasy of snow, found white sculptures by Gironcoli, <u>ach and snow-snugged</u>, and sprouting from my chest wafting age (but now it was as if tender nature had thrown her little arms around me, innocent lip upon which the snowflake melts, namely NUAGE (Fr.))

> .... I thought of you all winter
> and that you were in hiber-
> nation, you lovely rabbits squir-
> rels foxes .... and that you.

11.8.12

it catapults me, fate, namely .... <u>so monstrous</u> namely you smother me .... while the body of water that time when I was 1 child, how it shot out of the mountains, and I caressed the dainty fishes in its waves, back then the dreaming globe and wandering nights up the hills, &c.

mid-August the earth is cooling already it is cooling the earth white clouds periwigs ach darling how I rue your vanishing, embers of your heart just smoldering now your heart already shivering the morning already this shivering in the morning a lull, a hovel on the edge of the woods I dreamed the dahlias had died the lupines, still green the woods deeply shrouded shuttered passed away the fates, tears in the morning, my hand my mouth looking for you, they look for you, leaning on the window in the morning : memory namely the sweet, appeased globe, the moss with bare feet the moss and the dew the dew of the firs in the morning = the tears .... the dewdrops on your forehead : because you kissed me that time .... (it passes love it passes—like the changing shape of the moon : silver <u>colossus</u>, you tamp me into the dirt so I .... you tiptoe in the dawn day-moon pale colossus till it fills me with terror, terrible one, pale vermin, woe! you tiptoe over mountains terribly, I mean monstrously. As I, early morning, one-eyed, bedazzled at the window. Death, measured in spoonfuls, &c.

<u>and measured in violets, all your sm. shoulders</u> (gullet of the privet, bitter)

14.8.12

rivulets poured out, namely wrested am I, am mortal, ach rivulets whirred around, 1 wild petal on the lawn, ach sm. green leaflet grown into my finger there shall the pink buds unfurl, beloved, the brimstone butterflies, you know, the cabbage whites, in the name of the Sacred Heart, flaming, so like 1 Sacred Heart I say to my doctor, with thousands of rays and bouquets <u>on the display</u> &c., so that I froze, like he who was crucified, I say, while Martha Argerich on the GRAMO, heart impertinent, we strode through the woods &c. gullet of the privet bitter snow in August, final flower .... when I talk to you, I look into your left eye while it is swimming in blood, swimming in blood. I thought you were 1 evening-beauty, Madame, said Michael Heltau, pale moth in lush garden in August, Phoebus sinking behind the mountains like he wanted never to return, spilled ink evening sky, sea of flowers namely ach the little yellow blue and red souls of the night, night violas, primroses and poppies, tears of August, sea of tears in August deep drowning in tears ("Hercules") .... I mean I always have to cry hard when you. I mean rose-red the mountain peaks

it was 1 cold August day, my right foot (ached), <u>deep valleys and I was freezing</u>, so pear-yellow in the carrée &c. ach damnable girl, "sweet temper'd" = Marion Steinfellner .... somewhere at night in my neighborhood, windows wide open be it 1 table 1 chair 1 bed like Van Gogh's legendary image, fabled interior .... lambkins namely of a lesser home, <u>snowflaked woods &c.</u>, elderberry bush nights where finches namely in crowns .... you keep me company down all the paths, when one is old one wants to forgive everyone

19.8.12

of course because I was 1 child and timid she encouraged and consoled me, so later, when she was old I tried to give 1 little of that back, though without much success. She was 1 upstanding woman and she died alone : I came too late and kept the deathwatch and since then she has been watching over me I mean her grave, I visit it rarely

sometimes the air at the window in the morning is like the air was in D., I dreamed of a bouquet of violets it was dry and it rustled when I brushed it, mountain sputum, mountain sensation wasn't it so I sat in the pub garden pergola among young dark forms under the sun umbrella with wild rosebushes to the side, and pro-tégée nuages .... (as we were coming up the path from the woods to the street that time she skipped up to us, bending aside branches she wore 1 dress of wisteria roses little bed of singsong ....) ach you jet me into the violet-blue sky such a sea of flowers, I am buried under blossoms : taciturn little woods starry night of course that time in Venice with Klaus R., when he asked me in which church he should light a candle for me &c. "as if coming out of an almost secretive grotto," JD, remembered moss, tender branchlets in morning sky, ah murmuring poplars and CYPRESSES, 1 tat-terlet of lion and tuberoses scattered along the allée, if someone were to dapple me were to brush me while I am sleeping brush me with a little bouquet (of dragonflies) or were the moon to shine so brightly upon me I would wake up, flambéed bird, susurrating a little you know as we walked through the woods the branchlets SWAGGERED 1 bit while squirrels from branch to branch (kissing) cahiers and again "on the threshold of a Tibet" Jaccottet .... I'm a vagrant, the flower of a chamomile dunked in water, drifting through the morning forgetting the march of hours, days, as once in D., <u>praise god</u> the birdlets at the rivers fleurs and nuages, cedars in the bloody MOLINO &c., "all kinds of birds in it," it was <u>almost alchemy</u> that with the help of a flat magnifying glass, I mean that you could read something of your own handwriting, namely sugar-handiwork in the lush garden, like 1 lightning bolt the shadow of a bird flew over .... left eye : little pillow : squinting, such an edification : espalier of vetch, and thorn copses up on the fields at night, Martha Argerich on the GRAMO, &c.

22.8.12

last and final.

Then yes instead of an apple preferably a pineapple, while proof-reading the featherlet from the pillow at night namely my head plunged into the amorous bosquet, the friend of a friend at my side in white T-shirt through which the peaks of her breasts &c. on the green bed linens the red felt-tip pen, 4 o'clock in the morning. Little blond curls of the physiotherapist, late August and heat wave, back then in the wealth of curls of the jasmine bush plunged into an early spring long gone, crying. Piles of books next to the bed each with inlaid bookmark, Madonna! and dust-covered, late August: the swallows' farewell waltzes, noiseless the night without stars the black heavens, Cora P. with torticollis back then in the Kunsthistorisches Museum, pill sticks to the roof of my mouth, stepping carefully, in sleep the longed-for rushing of rain "étude" in the boughs, ring-finger recognizes blackhead on left cheek, smell of charred hair

(1 letterlet in the privy and flower-sea oh ....)

25.8.12

dumbstruck, I say, he was well-versed = went to the devil and then came back, the letter that should not be sent (trembling) from the mailbox to the floor, I mean as though it were meant to be lost, rapt eye-slits wooded bank gaping, as that time we hiked the steep incline up the Cobenzl hand in hand past oaks and upper meadows and stopped when our strength declined, etc. Threw myself into the sweet underbrush whereas you in the privet hedge pointed at the "Krapfenwaldl's" hills (red-blue funnel's) while the lump of moon = moon's, ach from the GRAMO : night tropes &c. .... with jags with wild jagged hair the philosopher or painter <u>with sneakers</u> and patientia ach rain-tears floated down on melancholy lawns ach <u>on</u> searing unsightly frozen bestial eye .... namely nighttime amid blowing fir trees, birdlets in tree crowns during summit attempt. Leaning on the window at night : <u>the night's</u> pattering, reading the otiose time, hour after hour .... he who writes upward, his hand : lines wandered WILDLY upward in notebooks, was eager to help always in a good mood it is said, that time in the hospital garden walking up and down narrow paths (I) cried, such an idyll, affectionate touching "bouche" your deep, light-blue eye oh it was as if my heart were compressing, (I) with stiff strands of hair, obstinately ONLINE, behind us <u>in black</u> <u>*look*</u> with ragged locks, whereas the news of the sudden demise of .... <u>blew</u> in. I write <u>*random art*</u>. Blossom-sea of a Dufy, once more wildflowers. Fleurs. My foot poultice, my tonsure, herd of ants in the WC, I had read 3 o'clock, thought it was 3 o'clock in the morning but it was 3 in the afternoon .... stomach acidic, see-slits inflamed, proëm from the same day &c. or flaming-red tulip field ("because we are enchanted"), rummage in bag crying looking for my keys, my nightingale : my hairdresser laughs. Late summer's halo, had delirium, had chest-antlers, had devastation, stared at the ceiling, insensate, <u>gala and phlox</u>, in which I went my way, imploringly, I see <u>garden maquillage</u>, the wave line of your mouth bouche, barefoot, the eye's TRANSIT, tussled hair, eruption of the forest bouquets, wild bird migrations 1 aeroplane, reading JD's "The Post Card" again, hardly leave the house .... foreboding, bluetit, must interrupt this writing

28.8.12

<u>Volker Braun's birthday</u>

I say to him in the evening, I can't tell any stories, but if HE pleads with me I will tell him a story tomorrow morning, the moon at its zenith while I'm at my nightly window, leaning, slim I mean waning (pining) autumnal already early fog cold morning, I say to him, <u>really great stuff</u> this prose by Volker Braun, I kissed him three decades ago in the Akademie der Künste, I say, *The Midday Meal* : Insel-Bücherei No. 1289, there's a <u>hype</u> around him &c., HE knows how to do prose, I say, skilled, Brecht, GDR, autumnal month— moon at its zenith, since I, nights at the window, sleepless, haven't seen him in decades now, oh (scrubbing) in the woods of the GDR that time, did I run into him there? can't recall his face <u>really great stuff</u> this prose by Volker Braun, *The Midday Meal* .... wolves at night : GDR, ultrasound of sensitivities, daddy's favorite, nights, sleepless, leaning on the window, Christa Wolf, Elke Erb, Heidrun Loeper, oh he knows how to do prose, 1 sacrament I say, as I sleep-walked, sleep-watched, reading his texts, etc., did not sleep tonight only read, read to the end *The Midday Meal*, September 1, <u>really great stuff</u> this Volker Braun, I spit at her feet I mean the GDR spitting at her feet dream elements of the previous night &c., green adornment in your eyes cuckoos in your chest, am not well read I rave about him, grains, narcissi, ears adorned with snails .... ach your Lady Fortune, "dark days are coming" (was 1 Blitz-girl back then), Martha Argerich on the GRAMO, am cuckoo, there's 1 <u>hype</u> around him = in the midst the lilac bush'es, shrouded branchlet .... in which I dissolutely, the path, the thing with the cherries, I have islands of order, the little red souls of the poppies &c.

3.9.12

John Dowland "*flow my tears*" and flying the whole time to Elba,
it's Indian summer, now. And was April and Easter. Pussy
willow still : bent in the glass : so swift, the moons and days fly
by, come my beloved to 1 late to 1 slaked sea reflecting September
stars, the lambkins (moving) homeward over the mountains,
"le kitsch," the full moon pours its GLORIA into the deep valley
.... we have forgotten a lot, for our life was very long. In our
dreams, memories, in our dreams we wander with Father Mother
hand in hand ("le kitsch"), and the end is chased away ....

red wavy line of your mouth how did I get so carried away and
WANTON, it was 1 pure full moon to call you on the phone, in
your belly button 1 dust mote Schikaneder, we hold hands and you
drag me along, so pear-yellow in Cornwall, in the warehouse of a
sporting-goods store for a few seconds it seemed to me, out of the
corner of my eye, Padhi F., what was he—what could have been
going through his mind for a few seconds when he saw me again—
presumably nothing very pure, oh! .... because we're enchanted!
OK we romped over the sloping meadow in R., dashed the full
pouches into the bushes, happily tore down the morning moon and
finally hung from its yellow tip. Diamantine from the sweetbush,
little petal in Türkenschanz Park, whispering secret codes, ach
beaten : bedded grass. I spend the evenings rather devastated. Oh
how alone we are now, said Traudl Bayer, and disappeared into
the bushes of Arenberg Park, where it was already dark .... but
it should all be very EXPRESSIVE what I supposedly want to
write, for a while now I haven't given two figs about the cahier
.... am *upstairs* : old hand &c., "because we are enchanted," my
arms are not the same length are they, 1 wanderer fantasy accompanied
me into 1 lupine allée I mean "the branchlets" are at the
heart of my fantasy / back then they would smoke on the top floor

of the hospital whereas Franz B. sent me the colorized photograph of a lupine holt &c. The invisible Loire, I say, from the glittering mountaintop someone called my name, saw that the moon, had hidden itself behind a gauze of tears (tatterlets of resignation green ornament in your eyes whereas the cuckoos in my chest). At 5 o'clock in the morning apparently 1 ferocious storm rose up and woke me, ah he <u>shat so kindly</u> since we were tailoring from the roof, namely the turtledoves were cooing this year is running itself to death already and it's only mid-September. You are 1 Taschist you have a snow-white memory, at last, he arrives with the scissors and cuts the letters for me <u>that have been arriving in dribs and drabs</u>

9.9.12

toute la lune : tore down, the invisible Loire but now it was 1 act of providence that on one of those sweet summer evenings I overheard the cicada's song from the ATRIUM, which left me shaking namely since I (glimpsed) green cicadas in your eyes now it was 1 act of providence that the glowing peonies the rhapsodizing phoenix the reveling eyelashes, beauty of the red amaryllis in the flowerpot .... meanwhile the provincial life. The landscapes fanned out and in my dream I wondered if Aunt H. were still alive &c., after her death 1 card had been printed with Dürer's praying hands, and I displayed it in my study ....

not the letter opener but the THUMB, I say, the unopened book pages torn open which seemed prole to me, JD *The Post Card*, my eyes grew damp, Francis Ponge, no sooner had this canvas fallen into my eye than I learned she was called Geri : after his death she must have found the letters I'd written to him in a passion (his cat's-face &c.), I felt so ashamed but she betrayed nothing, on the other hand I could have indulged in all kinds of debauchery .... after Jean Genet &c., in the meantime disgraceful unconscionable namely. And all along mediocrity was praised wasn't it, while in her bed the Traun : balconette or with ocular .... in my 8th year I had to do a recitation, was supposed to play Cinderella but my heart burst into bits and I toppled into the school pond, my broken heart hung on the trees in the schoolyard. Fluff and nonsense of the heavens ("*love me, love my umbrella*"), do we write *poets' poetry*?

16.9.12

"because we are enchanted" "how did I get so carried away and WANTON" "in which I the path dissolutely" (in Mariahilf.) Modern this Bristol thing like 1 transfer, the philosopher's steep upwardly panting handwriting ....)

"till the evening the breathing the flights the frights, let them go," "you comedienne," "these aches," "your blue eyes your chirping," "mornings hummingbirds in the hedge, " "the cumuli, you know," "dear child : you build into the clouds, you build ruins, into the water," "don't leave me ever," "hug me, kiss me, play the pianino," "when 1 cloud kisseth you, you won't feel any pain," "spreading your wings" .... very Olympic, Fontana : who cuts slits into his clientele, &c., am a ridiculous figure, I say to B., with my folded umbrella out and about, *love me, love my umbrella*, my mind is slipping away, behold! Blood streaming, my roof lair in the wind &c., <u>I mean the evening sinking</u>. Four months ago April I believe when the lilac bush, was still in bloom .... I take walks, you know, as we used to do, around the block when it is 1 warm day like in mid-September, exactly, and I buy you a bouquet of daffodils because you are so far away. That you certainly = ceremoniously with the car, we drove overland, 1x you dislocated my shoulder while helping me get out, hibiscus and amaryllis, the glowing summer just past as if it had a high fever, I knock the glass full of mineral water and it tips over, <u>my strophe God</u>, &c., would like to save my soul, bright-red Japan-book (Linde Waber), well it makes me blissfully happy .... <u>Doris has such imploring eyes, I say, perhaps gecko</u>, I swallow CRUMBS of Cenipres, start to

incur debt, ach senile : between 8 and 12 senile, &c. (he was a sky-
diver I mean the forget-me-not sky was his witness

"I'm no little heathen little angel
I'm 1 holy-communion-child, you
asshole")

20.9.12

"it was like 1 year, the two weeks were like 1 year, you'll see, the long hours and clouds float by, and the rain : tears down my cheeks (le kitsch) ...." Mannerism OK!, especially in the evenings : without 1 word, bent o'er thru' the streets, cold wind (le kitsch), you'll see, roses of June long since gone, swallows of May long since flown off, "otherwise everything's inside" Anne Lepper, invisible Loire, garden kitchen rhapsodizing phlox, I read the selfsame lines over and over, my eye is tired .... you have eagle eyes, he said that time as we crested the summit, and the scenery far beneath us was revealed .... sniveling a bit, even the littlest firs while in her bed the Traun, balconette in my dream meanwhile the new season, blows (whilom) tumultuously over sere crowns I mean. Where have the birdlets : sung away : flown away : whirred away to see-younever (who knows), profound gaze of a JUDAS, "in his study he had 1 REGARD, &c.," according to JD, it was the gloria the glacis of an alder grove, "the streets were dark, which was more than night, or, the closer I get to the end the more I rewrite the beginning," the elliptical sentences, the cherry thing, the unease, the garden-maquillage, CAHIER'S ....

in the dog park, in the Augarten, gentle mutts cavorted 1 bit while we, hand in hand, midsummer, spiderwebs in the hedges little pigeons in the woods, or Kahlenberg : silhouette of the city at our feet, we tried to find our stomping grounds down below, "there, the Ferris wheel, Prater, the AKH," scribbled with red felt-tip pen on white napkin, I say, because we didn't have any paper. The rounds beyond comprehension : gloss'd over in grammar : thither, fleeting, with apostrophe, &c., state poet of old, étoile .... these detours these many detours before one finds the right path which is headed toward the terrible end .... (drowning in tears, the mountains' rosy tips, always have to cry when you). The night's volte-face. Am cuckoo. This lilac bush, tatterlets of resignation, almost had to turn on the heat that cold August day (27.8.), skin of my hands : as if I had put on gloves that were too big for me, but now it was 1 act of providence, I say, these glowing positions of earth-life, the weight of enchantment, &c.

21.9.12

"those are symbols we were in Spain I was thirsty I mean to quench, in my nethermost belly, &c. Written like this, by hand, upwards, in runaway lines = Alexander v. Humboldt's address book. We're readying to depart, they're waving goodbye ...."

= waving goodbye

= the stars as they cascade down

so I hurried down the steep path strewn with carpets of spruce needles while behind me the naked woods, brown owl giggling, &c., my tonsure. I mean as I turned around (while running down : slipping down) I saw that the morning stood in flames, the morning light had caught fire and I spoke to Phoebus, how I shivered namely 1 delinquent, &c. Long after I had run into him = Otto B. at the Stockholm airport. I mean how I startled when I saw him, it was 1 sweet freezing, and I whispered, whither I goest, do you go .... lined with meadows the most frightening of nights couldn't fall asleep (till sedated) the fear that something might have happened, that in his moaning mania he might have just bolted into the sea = the water namely luring, hauling him ever more grimly into its deepest maw .... anyway, Carl Maria von Weber's Invitation to the Dance made me feel sick = *speed*, while 1 scantily clad tart darted across the street or, her ornament. And so I cried myself to sleep finally aided by a big dose of DEMETRIN which is a sleep-nudging medication, etc. This rule-of-thumb = bottom line, in flower-color, 1 inversion of the blossom = fleur (JD) .... ach between flowers and mountains or mountains of flowers, Thorsten A. sat in the phlox bushes that shimmered nights in the neighbor's garden : my FRONTAL LOBE responsible for the tenacity of my memories &c., "the magic's gone," I cried and implored the Kyrie eleison, adieu, little caplet! so ardent, gladioli your sweet swords (the casemates back then in the foxhole : Scholzgasse 16, 2nd district, gray ambience, transparency of a funeral cortège. It was 1 wan morning meanwhile, I had kept some of my ailments to myself but the doctor could read them in my eyes, he was very magical "and followed me into death," &c.

ACH WHAT CUSTOMS

23.9.12

"these confessions : tore down the moon à deux also sweetbush
little leaf in Türkenschanz Park, spend my evenings rather dev-
astated, it *is* all supposed to be very <u>expressive</u>, what I write . . . "

I mean fuel textiles <u>Fürnkranz</u> .... that night, 29th to 30th of Sep-
tember, was 1 guillotine blade, you know, agonizing ghost films
played in my head also en passant the <u>deforested</u> middle finger of
.... I mean how did it happen that I spent 1 entire night down
on my knees, praying on my knees = oh my knowledge of the
prayers was incomplete, ach let this night pass without terror. I
saw the fire-red amaryllis blossoms in the twilight of the night-
stand, you know, and in the morning I was done in, the night
seemed never-ending, <u>the demented shutters, &c.</u>, called every
half hour, but they always said, "in a trice," etc., tears flowed down
my face and suffocating, the worst imaginings, saw my beloved
tumble out of a speeding airplane into the trembling depths
adorned with sprigs of bougainvillea, like an air-burial, wasn't it,
while with my little wings (like 1 bird) I <u>in my depravity</u>, whirred,
I mean I *did* want to write very expressively about what stirred
me : which is perhaps 1 little old-fashioned, my pup .... the night
was still and the asterisk ✳ in the night sky, little star starlet 1
footnote = notified of a comment, &c. : in a sm. courtyard Prinz-
Eugen-Strasse 18 I stood with a little basket under my arm I mean
did I see the cherries and sun-fires in her arms = my orthopedist =
regardless I rushed up to shake her hand but she ignored it, <u>while
her beret</u> .... Erna Sack, as I was washing, this vagabondage of
my soul, but it was the everlasting abyss
"his sex was prodigious, <u>and while reading</u>, I held it in my arms
like the Christ child it lay in my arms, <u>and while reading</u>, it was

once again 1 affair-day, oh little redstart you tongue-heart! imagine,
this thin old woman totally horizontal with Bekhterev's Disease
SPEEDING across the street, with young roe deer and ravens,"
my cadaver, disgraceful. And mirror-inverted my entrails &c., mir-
ror of the heart, I thought, distraught, I was losing my mind, *hubris
of age* I took down in shorthand, half lying down : night-lying-
down, on the kitchen chair, wolfing down dinner, while in her bed
the Traun, <u>balconette</u>, or with lace DOILY

30.9.12

"well anyway, I was strewing thousands of flowers from the little basket stood with the basket under my arm in the courtyard at Prinz-Eugen-Strasse 18, I was carrying this basket strewing thousands of freesias, I mean as she, my orthopedist <u>with cherries</u> in her arms : had she, whose life <u>full of cherry-blood,</u> had she been shopping namely, I wanted to say hello by holding out my hand, but she ignored it (<u>ach this minimalism</u>) : had so much I mean had so much to carry .... haunted by such visions although it could have befallen 1 bit differently, e.g. Dufy's blossom-sea &c. .... so I hang around, look like a Down's child, look for words that have fallen, have fallen I mean into the bottomless pit, and I stare at that photograph depicting him with sm. pipe, crooked glasses, <u>and lost,</u> e.g. helpless in his last days so that it wants to dynamite my heart &c., and where was he VOYAGING : I turn up the GRAMO to "forte" so the little study bursts and my marrow bleeds oh holy nevermore (near' 13 years) I will never be able to hold my hand out to him again, my mouth, bit of a disordered shirt &c. <u>and little bones</u> .... gullet of the privet, bitter snow, ach (I) whirred like little birds. Like Rauschenberg. Your beautiful soul. Otherwise the exterminator will come, or the oriole .... in my dream I was melancholy, he wore a fashionable felt hat and looked like Minerva, grabbed my knee, I was <u>just about to,</u> I mean, fall in love with him : it was "Karli" = fallen apples along the highway to Deinzendorf, and when I showed interest in his dream-protocol he called out, you give me wings .... <u>lilac, for example,</u> MEANWHILE season blows over <u>balconette,</u> am abnormal, am philological, the Sacred Heart on the display. 1 fiery glow in my armpit, I let myself go to seed &c."

10.10.12

<u>what I whispered in his ear for Peter Handke</u>

as if I had scattered rice flakes into the fall morning anyway I found his mind moving and his words too I mean on that evening after HELENA's premiere party when I was the first to leave he got up and kissed me outside the tender strands of rain in April's abundance, &c., and in my suitcase on every trip his WEIGHT OF THE WORLD but then one day, I couldn't find it. When my Fr. friend Erika T. asked me what had occurred in Offenburg, where I got the Hermann-Lenz Prize and where I with PH I mean we danced to Ital. music, I offered: it was 1 epiphany. Well anyway I was monotonous : 1 child in love wasn't I, circa 28 years ago ah in the museum of the XX c. I crumpled his hands 1 bit : Otto Breicha's, before he began his talk, which I wanted to hear : while he, PH, stood between paintings, his eye coming to rest on me : only for a moment enfolding me namely oh what his eye was able to do just by looking at me, which was an étude &c. We sat with our publisher and Edith S. in the Sacher and I asked if he thought I was ungraceful : unlearned, which he felt was not untrue, which made me unhappy .... when, late in the evening, I took the car into the cubic woods and disappeared, he saluted me, standing on the street, goodbye : I used this scene for a text in honor of Sophie Taeuber-Arp. Due to new beatifications I FLEW up the steps of the Burg Theater .... ach little rivulet, birds were swirling all around

18.10.12

"<u>Maria Gruber : dumbstruck photomontage</u> .... during the night of the 5th to the 6th of October, which I spent sleepless in the hospital after an eye operation, I conceived my new book with the title IN A COUPÉ, at that time I was having a number of affairs as the 1st snow hung on the branches in the hospital garden .... in spring I had seen the chestnut trees spring namely white and pink candles .... (it is a lot to write "blessed child," one must stir in the salt of tears, sweetness of gloria, &c. you are my *sunny-boy*, Father always said to me back then, north wind undulated sun iron bars underbrush in the garden, lancet-shaped leaves diverging dotted with snow crystals &c., we lived in the garden, in the grove : robin redbreast on snowy branch, I mean I think I see there a sm. bird, blue and red, on a snowy branch : very sm. bird in white bushes : almost didn't see it because it was so inconspicuous in the forked branches &c. but then <u>endlessly</u> with maquillage and flowers of the air. Dreamed just 1 ringing of bells, and shadows, and sat just in a coupé, like Valie Export's *Knitting Madonna*, caressed the faraway pink cloudages while the floating snowy leaves revealed to me *The Theory of Changing Tones* (Hölderlin) = <u>such 1 excess</u>)"

24.10.12

"well anyway the bloom blossomed on her cheek to perceive this beauty more profoundly to remember this sea of tears more profoundly I turned off the light. As I stood at the door I remembered the bloom on her cheek I recognized the sea of tears in her eyes. To perceive this bloom on her cheek more profoundly to remember this sea of tears more profoundly I turned off the light. I opened up the writings of Francis Ponge I recognized Dufy in the gardens. As I stood at the door I opened the writings of Francis Ponge recognized Dufy in the gardens. Through the bars of a stranger's garden I sucked in the scent of a flower remembered the writings of Ponge recognized the scenery of the woods. To perceive the beauty of the scenery more profoundly to remember the bloom on her cheek more profoundly I closed my eyes. Arpeggione. Sonata. Franz Schubert. I drowned the ache in cataracts of tears let the year's 1st snowflakes melt on my tongue bathed in the bliss of your tears remembered the writings of the poet recognized Dufy in the tendresse of your dreams .... "le kitsch" = ach the longings 1 gesture of gloire ...." (THE LORD = THE SHEPHERD, had pulled the cloth low over his eyes "ecce homo" so the eyes could not be seen : painting by unknown master late 15th century) when he called with a darkened voice the tears welled .... "he pulled me toward him he yanked me toward him he kissed me," it seems to me I was 1 *FAN* of his, 1 plaything .... "I am worried I am worried I have not heard from you" Erika Tunner on the phone, I shoveled the roses the scent of the philharmonic orchestra into myself found my train of thought in the Mühlviertel, rancid. When you have felt the deepest pain of isolation you will be 1 poet under mini mimosa trees palms/pearls. The winter surprised us by arriving mid-October : winter boots buffed, reading very bad, crying? taking walks? How long does the ◉ need until it can see well again (street, risk) poor sight whitish light &c., early, from the window, antique tears very sm. spider : adorable sm. spider slowly on my books, on the floor. No, no diary just table-puppet = presentiment of death. Snow crystals at the doctor's office did I leave behind any flaps of skin flakes of skin. I mean 1 certain withering after the operation &c. (sm. agave : sm. bride, "oh, aim for her kitty!") piano solo "Cat's Fugue" Scarlatti as the agaves, sat then in the ZAUNER and ordered coffee mineral water am apathetic. Somehow the terminology of the checkup : fever sperm blood pressure faithfulness .... ach these lovers intelligence in the cahiers &c.

1.11.12

"well anyway, actually, declaim the bushes, he was fondling my garden, oh the enigma of a pear with a bite taken out of it, of an open door, of a dying flower, of a pair of forget-me-not-blue eyes (E.S.), the clock-face of your cognition, namely the terminology of the checkup : fever sperm blood pressure <u>faithfulness</u> (which drove me into the arms of my dead mother) .... as namely the agave = "courtyard full of roses," oh sink down to me night of love. It is the estamin, writes JD, Mother made a sweet little estamin dress for the hot summer days in D., to be fastened at the nape with a little pearl .... "narcisskirt," flight or thievery of swallows, JD .... as I spat at her feet, feved fevered, straightaway. Coiling on the bedsheet my eternally raining hair. As long as you are happy, I say to him &c. Possibly I can only express my thoughts through drawing and painting, sat then before Scarlatti's "Cat's Fugue" as the agaves .... do I still really feel that sandy knoll = <u>epicure's cheek</u>, flowers tendrils rockets, namely climbing the sm. knoll do I still feel the dust under my feet and the jackdaws' calls, pussyfooting a bit, or with Mother on my arm as the small dogs howled (Puchberg at the foot of the Schneeberg, back then, knoll that I climb <u>declaim</u>, the bushes for example, tiny snakes : snakeheads, which) .... with a wool shawl I cover my darling ear, which hurts .... fraught : caught : still in the weal of sleep I was not in a position to give in to the urge to drink 1 glass of water as soon as I awoke : still caught in my state of sleep I was not in a position, as soon as I awoke, to give in to the need to drink 1 glass of water : it would have been 1 audacity 1 rosebush. Sometimes (<u>lifelong</u>) one wishes 1 beautiful day would repeat itself, one wants 1 beautiful day to come back. The skyscraper of sm. cardboard boxes on my nightstand in the morning, just awakened from

dreams : just awakened from dreams : the skyscraper of sm. card-
board boxes on my nightstand ("NOVALGIN") .... <u>edifying</u>,
I'd curled up into a ball namely that time when I called Maria L.
she seemed determined not (to have) l talk with me I mean she
didn't seem to want to speak to me, which hurt. <u>Lifelong</u> : arrange-
ment of the folds of my existence, was I vain in my dream, did I
begin to read in the schoolbook of secrets .... I painted a wall
black and called out that is the death of EJ, crown of thorns with
black felt-tip pen quivered on the duvet, etc."

3.11.12

<u>to E.S.</u>

to feel at home in the friend's, blessings to
know where his, wings dragonflies meditative
cherubs, where his virtues lie dormant, oh his
good works, secretly namely the flimsy, fibers
of his heart, and <u>torn tears</u>,

4.11.12

A message of greeting, sort of, with sentiment

only this left : after the farewell to the unloved school
duties, back then, '69, only this left : this language, this con-
verse with my beloved German language which was my on-
ly HOME, you know, pressed to my heart till the
end, oh only this tantalizing clasp with my
language which is HOME : lachrymose, an apotheosis, a fren-
zy, a small chalkboard, a codex

5.11.12

am protegée, s'thing pearls in th' eye, the melancholia is already
roaring, "you didn't tell me good night," wasn't there hardly any
grass in the cherry trees : Thomas Kling. I've turned my back to
the world, the wind roars so fiercely over the small forest it will
burst : no, it will bow down under peppercorn .... stop crying
now my beloved, departed are my dreams, see how sparse the
crowns, the trees bowing down to the ground. Suddenly blurry.
Sight. Devil's bolete in the West, at 30° in the *bedroom* there's
knocking at the window, shrouded = wound in a howling wind :
November rain : gray blueblood, clusters of blossomsnow, I sit at
the window, rain-tears on the horizon. Well anyway dilapidated
hills, flock of birds. I'm one of them : wet, cold, ruffled feathers,
heavens streaming with blood. How is it, I ask myself, with whom
do I share this memory, can I say to you: "do you remember, that
time ...." or would it be better to ask someone who is dead ("do
you remember, that time")—but he won't answer (that time when
he stood in the doorway for the PHOTO SHOOT and waved,
etc.), boughs in the rain, a few weeds among the sweet william and
coltsfoot, ach how transparent these world affairs ("behold now,
I shall sleep in the dust: and if thou seekest me in the morning, I
shall not be" Cristóbal de Morales)

10.11.12

"because we are enchanted, à deux, tore down the moon also sweetbush little leaf in Türkenschanz Park, spend my evenings rather devastated, it *is* all supposed to be very expressive, what I want to write etc., sm. wooden shoes such a blossom-sea (Dufy), from the glittering tip of the mountain someone called my name, 1 lupine allée comes along with me .... you're 1 Taschist, have a snow-white memory, "the branchlets" in the epicenter of my imagination, tatterlets of resignation your eyes' green adorn(ment) .... I had imploringly gala and phlox, ach this ulster Father wore in winter, ach how deadlocked I've gotten in this life ach this ulster and WANTON, pink wave-line of your mouth ("bouche") : bare-foot sideways : little green leaves = fronds on thorny, branches praise god what 1 wonder, you know the little pail the cat drank water from. Occident Orient a note and on it an admonition : "IMMEDIATELY" : tacked to one little basket gauze of tears in the morning, on the display the Sacred Heart, twinkling .... we blackhearts snowed under with Cenipres .... back then in the park at Schönbrunn resting a little on a bench, because he couldn't go on, silent he was, then the allées in the park at Schönbrunn the heavy hovering birds I mean a little, sitting at a table 1 gauze of tears, that time in spring under the blooming trees that blew in the southerly breeze I mean this spring in white blossoms, right. 1 word too many one too few the duvet scribbled over with red felt-tip pen .... withered corncockles I mean nestled melted into your dear feet a few weeds boughs in the rain little pigeon between the sweet william and coltsfoot the sky, cobalt blue as though it were giving notice of snow, that memory (might be) knowledge of the future, blubbering on its knees namely snow-covered heart, well anyway in these weeks nature, notably, <u>undulated</u>, and in this way her soul was able to straighten up, presumably out of the bushes"

13.11.12

"namely as the lilac bush bloomed my parents went out to a bowling club I was still very small when my parents went out to a bowling club I remember I had no siblings my mother wore 1 tight-fitting short dress she was very beautiful and melancholy she had waved hair and cried often namely as the lilac bush bloomed I remember my grandmother on my mother's side sat me on 1 bench in the Rubenspark and held my hand, it was winter '27 I remember my grandfather pulled me onto his lap and started to play his concertina then I got very sick namely as the lilac bush bloomed I remember the world was painted in impasto and I was afraid .... this motto (was) incidental .... I remember namely as the locust trees bloomed and the dog Teddy came into the house I let it all wash over me and my youngest aunt wore 1 pleated dress my father seemed anxious and hardly spoke, no one read to me and no songs were sung, the moon shone onto my bed and the stars, SANK DOWN, namely gradually language blossomed and we ran in a circle as the lilac bush bloomed in the schoolyard I remember. All typewriters I remember, namely thought processes everything that fluttered off, namely ...."

14.11.12

"too bad into the valleys (and swift) undulated notably in nature, pressed flowers oh in a little paper bag ("dust"!) I found 5 mother-of-pearl buttons, tender <u>initiation</u> of my pale feet, namely the years were protracted : long winters springs summers, ach in my arms Phoebus in your form "gloire" &c. Descriptions of images cushioned, cheek, my dress is immersed in the street 1 gingko tree : 1 allée. To hide under my own tongue, I say, someone gives me : 1 rose petal, which seals my lips so I can't say a word .... ("JAZZ") adorable cur-semblance &c., seam of the heavens = headboard of your bed, Sir : come back, white dove, saw this fraying flowering moon consuming itself one winter night as we laid our heads together on the dais like flowerhead to flowerhead when we were tired. See the high-heeled snow-shoes in which Mother teetered through snowdrifts I mean along the snow-covered (Reisner-strasse) back then as hot tears I held my arms outstretched to her &c. I mean shabby sun falls ACCURATELY in Iris Allée at least in the case of the sword lilies = irises, they wafted in the winter wind over the threshold of the pastoral courtyard in D. &c., and when I entered cuckooland saw hydrangeas on the curtains a bit CREEPY dizziness in my skull <u>screeching birdlet</u> in the oncoming forest, am apathetic in this winterland, my blood is still everywhere the girl with pink lap, corncockles at her feet .... <u>I idolized</u> .... <u>he said (violet)</u>"

21.11.12

"pressed flowers in a book "le kitsch" &c. am servile as a dog have a sweet canine tooth the Jägerwiese you know the lilac bush that thirsts : lasts : dusks me, morning you know high spirits you know, albatross : royal wing-stroke of my hope was I in the allées of gingko trees (with numb heart) wasn't there hardly any grass in the cherry trees. Wondrous lip on lip like ecstasy silent accordance, I stuffed my face with the roses of the philharmonic orchestra &c., under the ash you know *under the ashtree* = which means *Aschen-baum* under the fever tree. Corncockles, unkempt, melting into your foot namely gladiolas their sweet swords, casemates back then in the foxhole : Scholzgasse 16 = Leopoldstadt where both great-aunts lived gray ambience : whenever a funeral cortège went by on the street below (seen from the window) they <u>washed them-selves biblically</u> .... now it was 1 wan morning that I welcomed I kept a few of my complaints from the doctor but he could read them in my eyes he was very magical and he followed me into .... fluff and leas "ach how alone we are" she called out that time and dove into the bushes in Arenberg Park, sm. wooden shoes such blossom-seas (Dufy) am protégée, am composing excessively, mornings, I'll be gone in a trice &c. with addicted eye (welling of tears) yellow bunting at your feet (such long tits) emotion from flowers, JD, I endure this disgrace, on the photo you always open and close your right eye, a few weeds world affairs, well anyway the dilapidated hills the flock of birds : before they sink down into sleep-trees pink silk-trees, well, the gloominess of her great wings, <u>screaming at things</u>. Talked about the summer which this time around we won't be spending in the mountains .... ADIEU, like lucky love that our hearts, we held each other entangled, caressing. Paper-thin bird the cuckoo in my chest, I mean 1 certain withering after the surgery ⟶ ach this groping around, they're heterogeneous my writings blubbering namely on my knees, rhapsodic with the accent on *raison* or reason. Empty plastic bottles swept behind the cabinet with my foot, half-lying on the kitchen chair : am already suffocating without an interlocutor stumbled then to the window THERE'S BLOOD IN THE SHOE or like garden-maquillage in murky air"

23.11.12

"am servile as a dog = qog (EJ) some how rain, he was called Little Woods ("Woody")—as concerns the contemplation of the woods : looks like a lady's beard. This moment is already definitive, you say, all lights gone out : in my neighborhood &c. we sauntered Sundays hand in hand across the emptied Naschmarkt, sometimes a few steps behind you : welling tears. Ran out of writing paper 5 in the morning pale sky I'm a Marxist, she says, can't pray, she says, sheer *pattern* .... the genii = roses withered in the grass back then and Marcel B. read a poem about genii, corncockles <u>poured out</u> over the meadow &c., <u>the chaises in the fire</u> .... the arts namely the splitting nails : splitting (= into the airs) : seagulls, how in the '60s we swam out to the buoys at the Adriatic Sea. Or in her bed, the Traun, frayed ANUS, we always have so many plans, you say, but then the day is much too short : we had planned to do <u>this and that</u> but then the day was once again much too short, when the asters = All Souls' the year is already ending .... no grave silence yet praise god : you can still swallow. Am a ruin am collapsed : pierced like needlework ajour stitch, otherwise everything's inside = Anne Lepper, saw sm. dog with hood, white-blue pheasant feathers on the tapestry Mother made by hand when I was 1 child &c. Thus wafting white handkerchiefs in left eye I hardly ever leave the house anymore ridiculous, you say, ants in the privy : they have sachets in their mouths backcombed hairdos Handel's piano suites from the GRAMO so ardently little caplet adieu (forgot to urinate) are you Christian are you a coach? You can't come in right now, black curl on the bedspread .... : because we are enchanted, à deux, tore down the moon = floated over the roof, petal in the Türkenschanz, do you remember, all those confessions .... since the forest floor on the KOGEL (our "local" mountain) in Winterbach was damp and we sank in because it had <u>rained</u> a long time and long had blessings <u>reigned</u> in the heavens, the photo that Nadja took made me shudder she sat in a hall of the Kunsthistorisches Museum with the painting, *Man with Golden Paw* by Lorenzo Lotto while I read my poem. UNBLOOD namely. Half-lying on the kitchen chair wolfing down food = <u>epicure's cheek</u>, without an interlocutor I was suffocating &c."

26.11.12

"pressed flowers in a book" : "le kitsch" &c. I acknowledge where he always did keep me company : came to breakfast at my place because I cried incessantly I acknowledge that I crush flowers, etc. am fully unfettered like snow the tremendous sheen, on your hair the longing for the pinks on the strawberry slope : how I am unfettered you *were* in the Alpine snow with the luminous flower-glow = snow-roses namely Ann Cotten's "To My Legs" lay awake half the night with little dove, to Albertina, I acknowledge that all snow-roses : they really had EYELETS you know from their youth on since the time of their youth lovely anemones in the pail in a tub e.g. it had rained the whole summer that time, ran into Ellen Hammer at the hotel door, ran into her again after many years, star in July heavens drifting in—we went on vacation together once somewhere in the Salzkammergut &c. I think at a lake she spoke of her childhood and that she'd <u>shoved in</u> small stones first orgasm dragged willow rods behind her .... dear Ann Cotten I found your beautiful poem "To My Legs" in a calendar am electrified &c., I wanted to sleep with him we went over to my former school stroked the lock of hair behind his ear (like Father when he would look at himself sideways in the hall mirror already silvery gray) I often draw for days on end fill 50 sheets &c., lie in bed almost the whole day : because only in my domestic environment am I in my right mind .... chest trembles sunken roses "le kitsch" and bouquets of pinks : it is a lot <u>to write blessed child</u> mornings in my cave as 1 flow'r that one shall never find again I plagiarize myself, Ann Cotten writes "To My Legs" we sat summers under apple trees while the brook burbled in the valley, shabby sun falls <u>accurately</u> in Iris Valley, I say, bury my face in a handkerchief or a cabbage leaf, don't I .... the moon's horn.

Smoked, steamed as streaks of cloud I see the high-heeled snow-shoes of my mother as she trudges all alone down the snow-covered Reisnerstrasse I have a kind of stop button in my feet, description of image cushioned, cheek, much-too-short life, I say, to want to hide inside a motto to want to hide under my tongue (oleander tree withering : did you spit on my remembrance? *weekend* in the *Glas*, corncockles <u>poured out</u> in the meadow, am a ruin am collapsed ....) uproarious associations <u>with greetings to Vienna</u> &c. 1 zephyr sleeps in my chest ach green adornment of your eyes .... ringlet's immersion" &c.

3.12.12

"churning upside-down in the morning are you SNAK ("and now the magic's gone") cataracts of tears, at night I talk to myself. The Helenental : white-highlighted on paper, he ushered me into the icons of humanity &c., considerate and calm ushering me into humanity's icons .... ach in my chrysalis of air, my lonely retreat of sheer purity of heart. The soul flies evermore : when I stand at the window at night chilled enveloped in a veil of tears, to the full moon = I feel how I ascend to the full moon : its splendor spreads over the breadth of the landscape &c., that's how my soul will fly in the hour of my death to the full moon I feel its cold garment enveloping me chilled while my beloved reels through his dreams : "you're an ornamental garden you're a flower in my ornamental garden you're a zephyr you're grass lettering you're light of heart" .... ache in the hollow of my knee bird-of-paradise flower on the ceiling (as if you had just flown in from New York, with your Burberry &c.), <u>when one is attached to someone</u>, I say, my arms spread wide, is it a canopy, someone gives me 1 rose petal it seals my lips so I can't say another word. This subtlety = upshot in flower color namely "in order to shear or gather all of the flowers" : JD .... then with snowflakes in my eyes I drove home, <u>slowly I am sewn in to Josef</u>, when I awoke and looked out the window I saw the horizon redden .... robin redbreast, ache you know as I sat and stared at the moon = the moon's train, there is justice to it, though it is painful, this becoming and passing away, ach my past <u>kindled</u> "when we f. I take off your : ⌐○═○⌐ " it knocked me off my feet, <u>my heartache</u> &c. = "le kitsch" &c., whooshed up. Ach my flowers and mountains, we sat in the asters (of the Loire) and Father photographed us (in the corridor), Thorsten A. next to the phlox in the neighbor's garden which SHIMMERED in the night never before seen such 1 shimmer .... that is to say, my cerebral lobes vicissitudes of memory &c., the Jägerwiese, you know, in childhood, it really did exist : we played ball, spruces and pines, Leopoldsberg we forgot ourselves, agony as from dying dogs, law of perdition, I say, you'll have to bury me I say and don't forget : don't forget me : you will have to bury me you can't get around it, then they'll all be singing like angels, I say, and I'll <u>curse</u> everything because I don't want to go because the Earth is still so beautiful : "because we are enchanted" because the Earth is much too beautiful for us to part from it, I say, law of perdition, my heart leaps so much do I love this life but one day like a soap bubble it will burst, what nonsense that we must go, hold me close, pansy's alms (psalmodizing) .... I wore my sneakers can you follow me then you called me on the phone and it sounded like it was from a great distance, eyne of the flowers, rivulets fall from the sky"

soft and dismayed your dear face as though from mock moons dewing clematis and periwinkle 1 branchlet stuck out from the image's edge, and we sat together under the apple trees in the valley, "<u>ardently little caplet adieu</u>," &c.

16.12.12

Translator's Acknowledgments

Some of these translations previously appeared in the following journals: *Chicago Review*, *Lana Turner*, *No Man's Land*, *Sand*, and *Still*.

The translator gratefully acknowledges the generous support of the National Endowment for the Arts, the Österreichische Gesellschaft für Literatur, and EÜK Straelen, and would also like to thank John Nijenhuis for his invaluable assistance in making this book possible.